52 WINDOWS in LIFE

HUMOR, HUMANITY AND HOPE

MARTIN KARI

Copyright © 2025 Martin Kari.

All rights reserved. No part of this book may be reproduced, stored, or transmitted by any means—whether auditory, graphic, mechanical, or electronic—without written permission of both publisher and author, except in the case of brief excerpts used in critical articles and reviews. Unauthorized reproduction of any part of this work is illegal and is punishable by law.

ISBN: 978-1-63950-346-9 (sc)
ISBN: 978-1-63950-347-6 (hc)
ISBN: 978-1-63950-350-6 (e)

Because of the dynamic nature of the Internet, any web addresses or links contained in this book may have changed since publication and may no longer be valid. The views expressed in this work are solely those of the author and do not necessarily reflect the views of the publisher, and the publisher hereby disclaims any responsibility for them.

Writers Apex
Gateway Towards Success

8063 MADISON AVE #1252
Indianapolis, IN 46227
+13176596889
www.writersapex.com

ANNOTATION

The book cover shows an art work of the
French Impressionist Painter
Pierre Auguste Renoir
(1841-1919)

In Loving Memory of Arja Kari

Behind 52 Windows into Life: Humor, Humanity & Hope lies a love that continues to shine beyond time. Though my beloved wife, Arja Kari, is no longer physically present, her spirit, laughter, and wisdom live within every word I have written.

This collection is more than a book—it is a tribute to a partnership that shaped my life, inspired countless reflections, and infused ordinary moments with extraordinary meaning.

May these pages stand as a lasting dedication to her memory: a reminder that love endures, that inspiration never fades, and that the truest stories are those written not only with ink, but with the heart.

CONTENTS

Acknowledgement ix
About the Author xi

1. Feeding The Chooks 1
2. Such is Life 4
3. Funny Things 6
4. Meeting the Python 8
5. Has the World Gone Mad 13
6. Neighbours from Hell 15
7. Falling Leaves 19
8. Reaching for the stars 21
9. One-Sided Phone Conversation 24
10. Space, The Final Frontier 27
11. I've Always Dreamed Of… 31
12. Motivation and the Process of Writing 34
13. Joy of Writing 39
14. One School Day only 40
15. Fire 46
16. Something Annoys Me 47
17. Fun 50
18. The Art of Writing, Its Rules and Realities 51
19. The Wheel Barrow 56
20. A Book and its Journey 57
21. Can 'Dugong' Stand for Caboolture? 63
22. Homelessness 66
23. Digging for Gold 3 Feet Deep 76
24. If Looks Could Kill 78
25. Sometimes When You Dream 80

26. Almost a Disaster 81
27. Nature's Cathedral 92
28. A Glorious Day 97
29. Golden 'Abitur' 100
30. A "Blind Chook" Finds its Corn 105
31. Christmas Once Upon A Time 111
32. Faces in the Street 116
33. Easter Bunny Surprise 118
34. Meeting a Parrot 121
35. To Be or Not to Be – That is the Question 125
36. Joyful Writing 127
37. "If Only I Had Known…" 130
38. The Postman 132
39. Smoking School Discipline 134
40. Father's Good Night Stories 136
41. "Don't Play with the Mucky Pups." 139
42. Love is Not Only a Word 147
43. Swimming Lessons 149
44. Finland and Alekis Kivi 151
45. Frankfurt Book Fair - 2012 153
46. My Book Fair Presentation 157
47. Who Would Have Thought… 161
48. The Girl Who Ran From… 163
49-1. The Hand of Faith – Part 1 165
50-2. The Hand of Faith – Part 2 167
50. Something You Should Know About Me 170
51. The Old House 172
52. Stop Worrying About Spilled Milk 175

The Beginning & the End of All Stories 179

ACKNOWLEDGEMENT

My special thanks to Janet Bestmann
For her qualified editing
She is also a member of Caboolture Writers Link

ABOUT THE AUTHOR

Born during World War II in Transylvania, Martin Kari undertook many directions in his life, starting as a refugee in Germany. Technical and then formal higher education prepared the author for life with a sense of exploration, adventure, intellect and humanity. Having worked and lived on four continents as a global citizen, he settled in Australia with his wife and six children. It was only in re- tirement that he found the time to take up the pen again.

Chapter 1

FEEDING THE CHOOKS

(aka, CHICKEN TALK)
Martin Kari

This story arises out of an activity that is both a hobby, as well as a means to provide a healthy food source for the family. I hope this story will please both reader and egg lover alike.

At daylight, the sun peering cautiously over the horizon, a cock-a-doodle-do announces the new day from the chicken pen. Shortly, after the rooster's call, all four hens also join in with their distinctive cackles. It is the noise of daybreak on the farm.

Granny Betty hears the sounds from the hen house, and says to herself, 'ah, it's time to feed the chooks.' Betty loves this duty, as she's a bit of an early bird herself. Sometimes the younger members of her household will occasionally help out with this task, so it can often be a good way to start the day doing something together-both young and old. Unfortunately, today, the young are not so keen to leave their beds, but Betty hopes eventually they will learn the joy of an early start and the completion of a satisfying daily job.

Granny, alone this morning, moves off to the chook pen. She doesn't want her 'darlings' to wait any longer than is absolutely necessary.

The bolt on the gate squeaks when it is released, and the sound becomes welcome music and a call for all the chooks nearby. The hens hastily rush to greet the 'feeding mother', while at the same time cackling loudly and flapping their wings. King, the only rooster stands his ground, he wishes to maintain his status with his girls, and moving to each hen in turn, he attempts to remind them that he is boss.

After Betty has locked the gate behind her, she calls to each chicken by name. She wonders if the chickens are thinking about their breakfast to come, and if they are thinking, is it in English, or a different type of chicken speak. It is very hard to tell, as there are no facial expressions as such to be seen.

Without doubt the chickens clearly understand the feeding routine, and the pleasure it brings to them. They seem to know that Betty will take care of the nearby empty feed bowls on the ground of the coop.

Penny, one of the inmates, seems intrigued with the use of the feeding scoop, and how much feed can be put on it at any one time. She seems concerned that there will be plenty of grain for all, but is also, at the same time, looking for extras. She likes those lovely green, fresh vegetables that are often strewn around.

Daisy, another hen, gives a completely different perspective. She appears to be proud of the eggs that have been produced for collection today. She wants Betty to know that there is an equal trade between the chickens and Betty, food for eggs. Eggs can only happen with a plentiful amount of quality feed daily.

King, the rooster, on the other hand, seems more concerned that the hens know that he is there, and that even though he doesn't produce eggs, is deserving of respect for the importance of his job as master of the roost. The hens however seem to ignore his efforts, after all it is Betty who is important in their lives.

Meanwhile, Betty completes her tasks: filling the two empty bowls on the ground with quality mixed grain; inspecting the water and then praising all the chooks for the four beautiful white eggs in the nest-boxes. 'You have done very well, I love you all. Before I leave, I will make sure your pen is fully cleaned of manure. I know you need to have good hygiene' she says fondly to her chickens.

So that there are no food fights among any of the hens, Betty stays for a short time. The birds peck hungrily at the grain, as if competing in a race. Occasionally a few drops of water is taken in to help the food go down smoothly into their stomachs, but mostly the focus is on food.

King suddenly chases one of the hens around the pen. With food on board, King has a renewed burst of energy and he is now interested in working out who is going to be his favourite in the pen today. 'I am the beauty in the harem, that is why he is chasing me,' boasts Millie the hen.

'Shut up, you are no better than we are,' the other hens object unanimously.

Nevertheless soon after feeding, all the chooks settle happily on the perch, not far from one another. Their eyelids don't know whether to stay half open or half shut. Peace has returned to the coop.

Betty farewells her pets, and calls to each by their name. She says to them, 'You all look well and healthy. There will be no need for me to call for the vet to see to you today.' She slips the gate bolt back into position, and enjoys the walk back to the farmhouse. A new sunny day continues for all.

The moral of our story: chooks fulfil the task of laying eggs, if they are well fed and looked after.

Chapter 2

SUCH IS LIFE

What is the purpose of human beings, out of all the other forms of life on our planet? A Chinese legend, partly from my own learnings and in my own words, tenders one possible solution. The legend has its origin in a remote area of the 'Yunnan Province'

Once upon a time, living creatures came together in small harmonious groups on 'Mother Earth'. When they multiplied beyond reason, however, the 'Creator' could see that there was a need for intervention. In order to control this development, the 'Creator' rearranged the lifespan of the creatures into units of years. No longer would lives be immortal.

Hence the first creatures received the one thousand year lifespan and as it evolved through the creatures, canines found themselves awarded 60 years, and the humans, well they ended up with a mere thirteen years. This was seen as a punishment for the humans as being overly interested in their own pursuits.

Naturally humans were not happy with this outcome. The best friends of the humans, the canines however decided to take the initiative, and ask the 'Creator': 'How can we live our lives which are so dependent on our humans, with such little time available for our human masters? Many masters during our lives will only spoil our good relationships, of love, loyalty and forgiveness. Your highness, please accept the dogs 'offer to sacrifice their years and swap with the humans. We will take on the thirteen years of our masters, and give to them, our sixty years. This would be so much better for the both of us.'

The Creator was truly touched by the canines' request, and responded, 'You dogs are so unselfish, and humble in your offerings. It gives me great pleasure to change the years offered, if it would bring you so much happiness in your lives.'

From then on, the dogs were happy indeed. As a result, from then on, on that one day of great changes, humans arranged a celebratory meal with their dogs at the same table as themselves. This was to recognise the sacrifice that had been made. On this day, it could truly be said, 'such is life', particularly from both the human and the canine point of view.

Chapter 3

FUNNY THINGS

"Where the heck have I put my glasses?" My day has kicked off badly already. I'm running around like a chook with its head cut off. "Helen have you seen my glasses?"

"Well, you're right. You are just like a mad chook. Try taking them off your forehead!"

"Phew, you are an angel. What would I do without you?"

I am reminded that the day has just started, and goodness knows what will lie ahead. I think that often it is the simple things that usually create the most complications. I hope I am proven wrong as the day progresses. Now that my glasses have found me, I can check the shopping list, and decide if everything is ready to get into the car.

We drove to the markets and completed our purchases as usual, but when it came to paying at the checkout, another problem emerged. Where was my wallet?

We hunted all through our belongings, went back to the car, returned to the checkout, but there was nothing to be found. We apologised profusely to the checkout girl, when we realized that we had obviously left the wallet at home.

"You're okay. Take your time. Your shopping will wait for you, and be here when you return," said the friendly assistant.

So it meant half an hour's drive back home to check the house. We searched from top to bottom, in both the expected places and the unexpected. We could not seem to find it.

Everyone by this stage was very hot and bothered. Helen decided a cool drink was in order. She opened the fridge door, and to her surprise the half empty shelves reveal an unlikely product. One very chilled wallet.

"Clever husband," she calls. "What is your wallet doing in the fridge? Who could the culprit be?"

Oh well, it's another half an hour's drive back to the shops, to collect and this time pay for the groceries. The day has truly become quite complicated from such a simple misplacement of one small object.

Chapter 4

MEETING THE PYTHON

Snakes have been embodied in myths since way back in history. The Egyptian Pharaohs used a snake embossed on the front of their crowns to symbolise their power. It was Satan in the guise of a snake that seduced Eve. The medical profession still uses the 'snake-symbol' today with the 'Staff of Asclepius' (God of Medicine) as their sign for medical powers.

In the 'snake-world', the Python is recognised for its power. So it shouldn't come as a surprise that our town of Caboolture has adopted its name from such a powerful symbol. We owe this name to the indigenous Australians. 'Caboolture' is literally the 'Python-Place' as demonstrated in its original name o 'Kabul-Tur'. The English language has adopted the original name of 'Kabul-Tur' to its modern version, 'Caboolture'.

It wouldn't be surprising to find there are many in the local community who do not know this fact. Moreover, it might be of public interest to find the name of 'Kabul' in Afghanistan, too. Could this shared name for the python indicate an early migration ?

The locals who live outside town in the Caboolture area can still experience meetings with pythons. An encounter with a python can only help to underline, in natural terms, the importance of the place where we live.

My wife with a python on our property

In summer, during the heat of the day, snakes absorb heat which enables them to become active during warm summer nights. It would be extremely rare to accidentally step on a python either during the day or at night. The python is a very cautious hunter and seeks its prey most effectively during the cover of night. It senses vibrations from the ground and the air along with the radiation from warm-blooded creatures. The size of potential prey must be indicated by the amount of body-heat-radiation in the environment because all snakes have poor vision and rely on heat-sensing to go after suitable sized prey for a feast.

Let me tell you about one of the many meetings I have experienced over a period of a quarter of a century since settling with my family on a rural property outside Caboolture. A birdcage near our house was, a couple of years earlier, home to some very special pets : one long-billed Corella, one yellow-crested Cockatoo, one Galah and an injured

Magpie from our area. They all got along very well with each other. Surprisingly, the smallest of them, the Magpie, played the role of boss over the others.

In the middle of the night, the repeated short shrill and extremely loud cry of the Corella startled everybody out of sleep. My wife and I knew from previous experience that a snake must have found its way into the birdcage. We had to explore what kind of thread this was. Hurriedly arming ourselves with a torch, a broomstick and a pair of large pruning scissors, we were quickly on the scene. However, we proceeded with extreme caution so that the unknown night visitor wouldn't turn on us all of a sudden.

My wife and I stumbled around in the dark, reproving each other to stay alert and proceed with caution. We directed the torch towards the birds inside the cage and what a surprise! A large snake had wound itself around the bar of a wooden perch which goes across from one side of the cage to the other. The snake's head was up in the air and moving dangerously forwards and backwards towards the frightened birds, which had all scrambled into one corner of the opposite side of the cage.

How could this snake's relatively small head (compared to its strong body) undertake to swallow one of the birds in the cage? And how had it got into the cage in the first place? The python's secret is that where the head squeezes through, the rest of the body elongates itself to also fit through. And when prey is caught in the tightening embrace of a python, it is only a matter of time before the prey's breathing will stop. The python continues to compress the prey with its body coiled around. Then the snake can enjoy this sizeable feast which it swallows by disengaging its lower jaws from the upper one, thus creating an enormous space for a feast of unexpected size.

We soon discovered that our pet Magpie, Maggie, was missing. The torch light was directed on to the snake. We saw the yellow body with brown diamond-spots and recognised it as a python. We knew we were in no immediate danger – not like with the king brown snake.

Quickly opening the cage door just enough to squeeze inside, I tried to distract the snake and lure it out of the cage. I stirred up the intruder with the broom handle. From a quick first guess, the python was at least 3 metres in length and therefore one demanding respect. We continued to make a noise by bashing the broomstick and in fact, the noise, the light and the bashing obviously deeply disturbed the python. It retreated first from the wooden perch, untangling from its special grip and moving in an increasingly straight length towards the cage-mesh and onto the ground.

Our presence must have disrupted the python's plan. The broom finally ensured the python's exit from the cage. It became obvious the centre of the snake's body was enlarged. No doubt, it was our missing magpie which, with its innate curiosity, became the first victim to learn a python lesson.

The gap of the slightly ajar cage door served the python as a means of escape. Outside the cage, it disappeared into the dark night with the speed of a thunder bolt. What remained were the other birds in the cage and us, shaken to the bone with a mixture of anxiety and satisfaction that this meeting with a python was over.

Not much sleep was for the rest of the night, not just for us but for the birds in the cage as well. They remained vigilant in case the python might revisit them. However, the python that has had a feast will, in most cases, not be able to squeeze either in or out of where it managed to get through before.

The following day, we were able to examine the birdcage for larger than normal holes in the mesh. In a shed on our property was some spare wire mesh stored away, which I went to fetch. Near the mesh, also stored away, was a cardboard box. On inspection, it was revealed the python had taken up residence. It was tightly rolled in a spiral, resting and calmly digesting what was most likely not just our magpie but other creatures swallowed from the last night's campaign.

The thicker part of the python's body indicated that more than a magpie had found its way there ; maybe even a whole mouse or rat family as well. The python in the cardboard box looked peaceful and content with digesting last night's swag of creatures for a number of coming days.

On the other hand, I was stunned to watch from so close a peaceful python. My wife arrived on the scene only a little later and could share this exciting experience. We were even keen to caress the python body very gently with our fingertips, all the while ready to retreat in case of disapproval by the python. Surprisingly, our touch didn't upset this impressive creature at all. Rather, it looked at us calmly and friendly as if it knew our feelings.

To meet a python today remains a privilege nature shares with us. Everybody who can experience this has a reason to be proud. We all should be proud that our town carries the name of such a magnificent creature, the python.

Chapter 5

HAS THE WORLD GONE MAD

Mr. Positive and Mr. Negative have a beer together in their local pub. It's late in the afternoon, after a long day's work:

'How was your day?'

'If I complain, nobody listens, and they couldn't help anyway!'

'Well it can't be that bad; you still made it to the pub.'

'Oh, drink up. I'll take care of the next round. What do you think of those politicians granting themselves a pay rise? More than we could ever dream of taking home. Do they even think about us?'

'Isn't there a saying which answers your question: If you can't beat them, join them? I don't have a problem with the bastards, I don't want their job. I'm quite happy with what I've got. Would you like to be in the cross-fire as they are?'

'I need another beer. I can't believe you. What if everybody let them off the hook like you're doing. Where would we end up? The bastards would fill their pay-packets with even more money.'

'What's the use of worrying about something we can't change? By the way, how are your wife and kids going?'

'So long as I bring the pay home every week, no one's complaining. However life is getting tougher to make ends meet. I wonder if it will ever change for the better, or just keep getting worse.'

'Ah, I love my family, it's everything for me. I just take things as they come, and try not to worry too much about the cost of living, otherwise life would be one constant worry.'

'True, you are right in how you think. Talking is one thing though, but coping with the down-sides of daily life is not so easy. I feel like we just can't win anymore; just look at the bills. There are some in the post every day. Since when are we supposed to only work, to pay the bills – it's Council, government, and everyone else who wants my money.'

'Yeah, your right. C'mon, let's try to look on the bright side – have another beer. Look we're both rugby fans right. So how about coming to the game with me tomorrow? Our families can have a barbecue together at my place, and then off to the game. How's 3pm, that'll give us enough time before the game starts.'

'Oh, you've made my day. I love the footy. I'll let you know after I've talked to the wife. I'll bet she'll be up for a barbecue with the kids. This is better than talking about the serious stuff of life.'

'As a friend, you need to know there are two ways to look at something. Take a half-filled glass of water: one bloke might look at it and see just a half-empty glass, whereas another bloke would see the glass merely half full. You've got to forget about the madness in the world, and focus more positively. Get positive with that half-filled glass of water.'

Chapter 6

NEIGHBOURS FROM HELL

Neighbours by definition are near inhabitants. It comes from the Celtic language, as well as the old German 'neah- gebur'. We all live with neighbours in some form. The only difference can be that they can live close by or further away. This all depends on the area where we are all living.

A lot has been said in relation to people living as neighbours. One of the key factors is the space between neighbours that essentially drives their relationships. People living in large housing units where the neighbours are cramped for space on top, beneath and beside are the closest neighbours. Interestingly, despite their physical proximity to one another their neighbours live at a distance relationally. Often these neighbours do not even know the names of the people in their immediate neighbourhood. Contrary to geographically close neighbours, people who live further away from their neighbours can have closer relationships, too.

In order to further understand these apparent contradictions, let's look at some examples from both camps: the close and the more distant neighbours. First of all, let us look at the sorts of things that can impinge on our close 'neighbours'. Many of us have experienced some of these issues in the course of our daily lives.

- toilet flushing after 10pm
- television and radio above 'room only' volume levels
- parental supervision of children
- designated parking area only for tenants
- towing away of unlawfully parked cars
- advance notification of parties, with tenant consent required
- no pets policies on estates
- noise limitations affecting lawn mowers, musical instruments, motors
- guaranteed investigation of complaints

So what things cause ordinary tenants into the 'neighbours from hell'? Most of the time it's heated verbal exchanges, which show little empathy for the circumstances of others:

- keep to yourself and mind your own business
- don't park your 'crap-car' in my area again
- keep your kids away from my washing, or I'll give them what for
- keep your noise down
- you're nothing but foreigners
- I've been here longer than you
- an outburst of 'quiet' from the flat below is reinforced with the knock of a broomstick on to the ceiling of the noisemakers above.
- the phone rings, 'shut up, I need a rest!'

Neighbours keep an eye on the goings on from behind drawn curtains; feel they are learning about others. A squeaking bed in the next flat might be the sign of a good relationship developing, but it can also prevent others from a good night's sleep. However colourful imaginations can also give poser to the spread of false rumours, which can quickly sour good relationships. These then turn those involved into the 'neighbours from hell'.

If neighbours exchanged words in a much more considered manner, how different their life together might be. How much less stressful things would be. It has to be so much easier and less controversial to either say nothing or simply go next door to discuss things using kind words. To allow one's neighbour to meet on a friendly wavelength, even just five minutes of kind words would be helpful. It is so important that people can offer each other support instead of useless, negative remarks.

For example, what would the outcome of a neighbourly interaction like this be?'Good morning, what a beautiful day. Isn't this a day for the beach after the lawn has its haircut?If your mower is still causing you problems why not use mine until yours is repaired?'

'It's not that easy! What if your mower blows up while I'm using it? Will I then have trouble with you, as well as the mower?'

'No worries! If this happens come over, we'll have a beer and try to work it out. There is nothing in this world we can't fix by talking it through.'

So the neighbour's lawnmower is borrowed, and then returned, possibly not in the clean state it was lent. This is ignored; the neighbours have a beer anyway. Far-sighted is the preferred option over short-sightedness in dealing with neighbours.

Geographically distant neighbours on the other hand, tend to heave less strained relationships. The distance allows every exchange, time to cool down before it eventually arrives. As the growing world population moves closer together, we are becoming unavoidably closer neighbours and need to learn to respect each other instead of consigning ourselves and others to hell.

Neighbours are there to be respected. We must avoid questioning outspokenness of one another, and reflect on our words and actions. We should be able to recognise that it's never only one side, and the aim should be reconciliation, not wishing someone to hell.

Literature reminds us, 'we should all love our neighbours.' In the real world, life happens where by words and actions do not match, and can often cause conflict in relationships. There is no need to dispatch anyone to hell, especially as we would not like the consequences of such actions.

Let us step back a little from our 'egos' and consider others from a distance, before jumping to conclusions too quickly. We know that behind everything said or done, there is more to be learned. The more time we allow 'a hot soup' to come off the stove and then onto the table, the more it can cool down without burning anybody's mouth. Neighbours can act like good neighbours, and not the ones from hell. If others do not behave in the way we expect, there is no reason to argue heatedly. Is it always the other side that deserves 'hell'?

Here are a few proverbs that reflect on our dear neighbours:

- Good neighbours need no fences
- Pay attention to your neighbour but keep the fence in any case
- The neighbours' kids are always the bad ones
- Two bad neighbours mean relentless warfare
- Love they neighbour as yourself (second commandment)
- What drops into the neighbour's garden is his
- A good neighbour is a jewel in one's own crown

It depends very much on us as to which side of the neighbourhood conversation we lie. We can either have a negative or a positive relationship with our neighbours.

Chapter 7

FALLING LEAVES

(poem-Martin Kari-2015)

Winds are blowing, leaves are going,
From close and far they whisper,
The eternal melody of changes.

Spring finally brings again a start,
Into new life during all mighty summer,
First with tender buds.

But then opening into nature's roof,
Primarily green and dense,
To give shelter and shade during summer.

Gentle breezes, fine perfumes,
Life's veins of water and warmth,
They all escort new life into the next change.

Snatching into the beauty of autumn,
Leaves decorate now colours,
To a farewell or a show.

But who should benefit from it ?
The leaves still whisper the melody of change,
What has been created, is passed on.

Again the hopeful little buds,
They come to life,
And the Old must give way to the New.

The old leaves finally leave the branches,
In a last charisma of a beauty,
They sail supported with wind to the ground.

Only to pause in a carpet,
Once more colourful,
Until fate of change has caught up with them.

Sometimes feet, hurried wheels on the ground,
Assist the change of the leaves,
Into a colourless new look.

Mother Earth has brought to life leaves , too,
And there is no escape,
From returning to Mother Earth less charismatic.

REACHING FOR THE STARS

'Reaching for the stars' – does this mean looking for the brilliant light of a star in the sky? Is it something for which we strive that is high above our reach : something after which our longings and wishes struggle? When our own expectations distance us from reaching 'higher ground', we then salute with enthusiasm the one who climbs onto this symbolic 'ladder' to the top to become a star.

Already, from early childhood, we look at something new in amazement and this feeds our imagination, often creating the stimulus to strive also for it. This can be all sorts of goals to become: a high speed train driver, a race car driver, a soccer player, a cricket player, sometimes also a performer of music, an astronaut, a mechanic, a nurse and many more, depending on an individual's private dreams.

Who hasn't cherished such aspirations? Throughout life however, we all experience highs and lows in achieving these dreams. Ultimately these highs and lows set us apart as an individual in an ocean of so many others, just like ourselves. Only a few make it to stardom, while the vast majority can only watch, hope and keep wishing to better themselves.

Most of the time, a star is expected to show to their fans, a mirror. This mirror reflects back to the fans the success that's been experienced. The mirror shows an image of the individual's dreams - their real hopes. This says this is what stardom is about. The response of the fan is seen in visible outpourings of joy, high energy, yell and screams. For the quiet achieving fan there are less showy effects of excitement.

Once declared a star, the attached expectations of stardom usually run very high, often leaving the 'star' at their peak in a vulnerable lonely position. The Brazilian, Coelho, has expressed just this in his recent book 'The Top is a lonely position'. Having reached the top, the star's position brings many expectations to live up to, perhaps to go even beyond what has already been achieved.

Human stars, just like their counterparts in the sky, can disappear very quickly, especially if the continuous expectations of their fans are not met. So much depends on maintaining the success, which has built up over time.

Where does this leave the 'little fish' like me, and those like me, who desire to move up the career ladder? Certainly, there is more than one way to reach for the stars. Looking at those who have already made stardom, it can appear that they have had luck on their side. However, I and others, we will just have to 'bite the bullet' and work so very hard to even get near that ladder to stardom.

What does the reality of climbing the success ladder look like? Most of the time, established stars don't dwell on the difficulties on the way up the career ladder. Once the broader public confirms a star's position, it is the performance that only pleases and satisfies. Left behind is the scaffolding that helped build the star's performance.

On the sometimes rocky road to becoming recognized as a star, many things can be encountered : support, jealousy, joy, disappointment, success, defeat, hope, despair, progress and setbacks. Nevertheless, as in everything else in life, the means determines the outcome. It is only the person who can overcome most hurdles who can look forward to achieving their goal, even if they are taking small steps.

A star has to deliver what the majority of fans cannot even express. This delivery can be either showy in a public way, or in the determined steadfast performance of the quiet achiever. A good example of this would be the entertainer Michael Jackson compared with, the considered performance of the American President, Barack Obama.

In some cases, we see many star performers who are 'fly-by-fighters' emerging from the masses. These are quick to be seen, and then equally quickly, to be gone. A star that shines for the longest period however, relies more on a lot of hard work, to achieve and stay at the top of the career ladder.

Finally, I would like to refer to the comments of an Australian icon, R. M. Williams, who said: "I am not as smart as many others but I work harder than many others." R. M. steadily climbed his way up the ladder. Everybody's life is about hanging on until the last man clinging to a thread of rope becomes the winner. Shakespeare said it best, "All's well that ends well". So it is with the stars; the one who prepares well, is likely to become a recognised star, shining above the mediocrity.

Chapter 9

ONE-SIDED PHONE CONVERSATION

"Gossip straight from the heart"

"Hi, it's Martin calling. I haven't heard from you for quite a while. I'm just fine, as always, so don't worry about me. It's the weather that is getting to me lately. My house needs work done urgently to the roof, but because of this heat, I'm sitting inside trying to keep cool. This 'bloody' summer! Truly you wouldn't have a clue what it's like to work on a roof. It's like the heat from an oven mate. It's enough to cook you. Nothing gets on top of the heat, neither your hat, no matter how big, nor drinking cold water constantly is enough. You wouldn't even think about a beer up there. Of course, at work, it has to be straight water out on the 'esky'.

But wait a 'sec' (second), this wasn't the reason I phoned. Last time we talked, you mentioned that your neighbour's wife was sick. I bet you've heard more than your share of 'kid-problems' from the husband while he's looking after them. Spare me those stories. You know I can't figure out how as a family, they manage to drive a flash 'Holden Statesman', and as well as having other cars to drive. The others, from what I've seen, don't look too bad either. I couldn't afford them. I bet all this is owned by the bank!"

After a brief moment to take a breath, this rather one-sided conversation continues.

"Hey, by the way while talking about the bank, you wouldn't believe what I've heard about our bank manager. You know how we've been with the local branch of the State Bank for years. They've been terrific, always helpful, especially the manager. Well, when I went to town a couple of days ago, the manager was not to be seen, and I heard that he'd got the sack.

Isn't it amazing, even though we don't see each other, we can still talk on and on. The weekend is only two days away. I've nothing planned so far, but the beer is chilling in the fridge, and the barbecue is ready to fire up. When you come, make sure you bring something to share with our two large families. Make sure you bring everyone; we'll be able to listen to the cricket tour of Australia in South Africa. I'm sure this time round we'll teach them a lesson.

If the weather turns bad, we can always move into the house. What do you think? Hey, are you still listening? You're very quiet. Are you still on the phone? Of course you are. You like a good story about what's new in the world.

By the way, don't you think life these days is getting harder? Just when I was leaving work today, I noticed the boss didn't look too happy. I know he's worried about getting work in at the moment, I guess that's taking its toll on him. It's anybody's guess what the future holds. But why worry? There is not much we can do. What goes up, must come down, and then it goes up again. So the cycle of life goes, unfortunately. I don't think life will change in a hurry.

While we're talking, I've been also thinking about my visit to the dentist. I hate the dentist, mainly because it hurts twice. First, there's the treatment, and I hate the sound of that drill, but then there's the pain in the wallet, as well. I think I'll wait and see this 'mouth plumber' after our barbecue. Who wants to spoil a meeting of mates with a trip to the dentist?

Now it's only up to you to say yes for this Saturday. What do you reckon? Isn't it a great idea?"

'Well, you've said it all, so I guess I've only to say yes!'

"I knew you'd like the idea, nothing gets in the way of mateship. Hang on, the family have just returned. I'd better stop chatting before I'm interrupted out of the blue; you know what it's like after the wife and kids have been out spending your money. We've agreed on Saturday around lunchtime for the barbecue. See you all then."

Chapter 10

SPACE, THE FINAL FRONTIER

Not so long ago, theorists could pay with their lives at the stake or guillotine, when looking with a thirst for knowledge into space. Out there, away from 'Mother Earth', was then understood as divine territory. Still in the 16th century, the idea was upheld that the Earth was a disc and we had to be careful not to go too close to its perimeter in order not to fall into endless space.

The early natural scientists, Galileo Galilee, Copernicus and Kepler established that Earth was not the centre of the universe, and that everything in space revolved within a complex system.

Galileo Galilee had to, however, confirm his absolute faithfulness to the Roman Catholic Church and deny his doctrine upon oath. This was so he could escape torture and imprisonment for his beliefs about divine territory. Galileo however is said to have exclaimed on his deathbed: 'Anyhow, it is still moving!'

Today though, such knowledge is taken for granted, and has largely driven out ignorance and the power to uphold it as truth. How far indeed have we come in the 21st century?

In 1969, mankind trod on the surface of the moon for the first time. Radio Astronomy enables us to penetrate deeper and deeper into our universe's space. The more knowledge mankind obtains, the more the unknown confronts us. In addition to this, a desire to expand man's power pushes us to leave 'Mother Earth' territory.

Science and technology enable us to search further than we ever thought possible. We can use time to measure our existence, because time is of our creation. However, space is infinite, and beyond our distance measurements, and our comprehension.

In space, astronomers talk in millions of 'light-year-distances' to describe distance. They do not use the term kilometres for distance. The term of space distance refers to the distance an energised light beam travels in a set amount of time. For example, the energised light beam travels at a speed of 360000 kilometres per one second. We might search in the space of the universe forever, essentially neglecting our home territory, 'Mother Earth'. On one side, we create fantastic technology preparing ourselves for our next trip beyond the Moon to Mars, while on the other side, the infinite space of the universe might well laugh at us for such futile endeavours.

We must ask ourselves; do we run the risk of trying to reach for the stars, while the outcome means we must neglect what is closest to us?

Certainly, progress in space gives us more understanding of our lives back here on Earth. New learnings from our outer space experiences, such as nanotechnology, impacts on medical science, new material compositions, and eventually new ways of energy transfer are the results of our unlimited thirst for knowledge.

We know too well, however, when there is progress there is always something else left behind; or, where there is 'good', there is also 'bad' to accompany it. In other words, polarities are the incessant companions in our lives, and where does such a rule come from? Out of space!

Everything in our universe's space is controversial for us. While pushing frontiers further, we confront controversy in exchange. For example, communication satellites out in space connect us around our world. The controversy lies between the dependency on the satellites, and the inherent vulnerability of such progress.

At the same time it is a race on Earth to dominate using hidden out-in-space weapon systems. What prevents this from becoming a reality is probably the fear of the impact of this on the world as a whole.

The first signs of a space race already evident are the increasing horrendous amount of space-junk circulating in Earth's outer atmosphere. These are the remains of our space explorations being dragged slowly back towards Earth's gravitational field. This shows that what is sent out into space meets different conditions to those on Earth.

Space junk increasingly threatens the International Space Station, and is becoming a danger for air traffic. What goes into space requires tight control to avoid becoming an uncontrolled menace when returning to whence it came. Luckily, the Earth-atmosphere shields us against lots of space-junk, mostly by burning off on penetration. Larger space-junk can however travel incompletely burnt through the atmosphere and impact with high speed unpredictably anywhere on Earth.

Nowadays, serious plans are taken into consideration to develop technologies which also collect space-rubbish. The interesting part of this is that we have to learn: it takes the same amount of effort to return something from space as to send it up there. In other words, efforts to get us out into space equal the efforts to return to Earth. Therefore, it is not good enough to get out into space without proper preparations for a return; that is if we want to keep some control over our actions in space.

The cost of space exploration has become so incredibly high that we need to consider justifying the cost, if its purpose is only to maintain reputation within the international community. A redistribution of 'space-money' on Earth could solve this current dilemma. But then again, where would human exploration-intellect be left?

We need to look closely at our reasons for researching to space. Are we looking into space only because of insecurity in answering the challenges here on Earth? Are we looking for an escape route?

Primarily, the challenges for us remain here on Earth. So much is left to improve, issues such as widespread poverty, equal opportunity, and concerns regarding Earth's environment, are to name but a few. Wouldn't we be better off to concentrate more of our efforts on our home ground, before trying to reach out into space, the final frontier where we can never reach an end, and running the risk, therefore, of becoming lost?

As long as this focus remains only under discussion, space will remain a testing field for us. Let us ensure we are not left without a future behind on Earth, by shifting too much effort into endless space.

Chapter 11

I'VE ALWAYS DREAMED OF...

Aren't dreams like bridges across a river to another shore? Let us find out how to travel a dream eventually to this other side.

It is said that daily life must be a struggle for dreams to be born- a case of 'no gain without pain'. A known fact about dreams is that they have a very short time frame. However, they can often have far reaching effects on an individual's life.

A dream is the bridge waiting to lead the dreamer across to another shore. How this happens in one's life is best shown as three pathways: one can succeed, one can remain in limbo, or one can fail.

a) The best way to depict the first dream's pathways would be to reflect on a personal experience of mine that has succeeded. The adversities mostly during and after World War 2 had turned my focus towards an escape from the troubling experiences of my early childhood. One of the early books I had read many times was the life of 'Robinson Crusoe' set on a deserted island. Even though I couldn't relate to the hardship of such a life, what remained was understanding the longing for a more independent, and simple life.

   In search of this outcome, I went through many stages on this pathway. Only perseverance crossed the bridge to the other shore, when Australia accepted me at the age of forty, and my family, as migrants. The efforts to make the dream come true didn't stop there, but rather continued under different conditions from what had initiated it. The dream of independence has become largely a reality. We have been living for the past thirty years in harmony with the natural environment, creating our own 'paradise'. It has also become the platform, where I started writing, thus developing a new direction in my life. Here, a dream has helped extend life past present boundaries. We have arrived on the other shore.

b) Now, what is the in-limbo dream? Let us look at 'Peter', a grade 10 school boy who lives in a small country town in the State of Queensland. Unlike his older brother Michael, Peter is rather less outspoken, especially at home. This, however, doesn't stop him from occasionally expressing his dislike for school.

"School is boring! I wish I could do what I want." His parents, on the other hand, admonish him emphatically, and repeatedly. 'You need to complete school, and then your dreams can come true.' Peter, a good kid, listens to what his parents have to say, and follows their advice for the time being. He keeps however, his wish to become a star tennis player as a secret treasure. As long as Peter attends school regularly, his parents have no objection to their son's tennis ambitions, even when he spends more time on tennis than the parents would like.

In contrast, though, a friend of Peter's from another class has taken his dream to be a star tennis player, into his own hands. As a result, the friend finds himself trapped between school duties and tennis.

The secret behind the dream is to give it time. No dream can forcibly succeed. Like everything else in life a dream pathway has its own traffic rules. The most important rule is to keep the eyes open when a dream receives its green light.

We also have to acknowledge that everything in life is accidental, which means, grab a chance when it is offered. Peter realised just in time, that it was better for him to avoid the in-limbo pathway of his friend, and to make school his priority. Tennis is not running away for Peter, because only time will tell how he can maintain his tennis dream in the future.

c) The last pathway for dreams is failure. This is often taken on board with the company of luck. There is a rule here also. He, who pushes his luck, is closer to failure than the one who allows time to work for his dreams. Examples of this are Lotto and gambling.

Failure is the dominant option here, because chance greatly outnumbers wishes. When a dream catches up by the pure luck of one in a million chances, such gains are more often short lived because everything that lasts operates on another imbedded rule: a quick win on a fast lane is likely to become a quick loss or failure.

In closing I wish to highlight a finding about dreams. Dreams are our 'castles in the air'. They hold a secret which asks for time and care, so that these 'castles' can land on solid ground.

Chapter 12

MOTIVATION AND THE PROCESS OF WRITING

Your mind is a garden, your thoughts are the seeds,
you can grow flowers or you can grow weeds

Now, why motivation first? Before the process of writing can start, motivation needs to be in place. Who is the bearer of a said 'motivation'? It is no one else but us.

Motivation requires a restricted focus on something we want to express or do. What gets you motivated for writing? What would a right or wrong motivation look like? Generally speaking if play with words occurs, motivation is there. The right and wrong is up to the writer, and reader to decide upon.

We all know quite well that good writing is created neither in a hurried or busy environment. The writer needs to think about where they like to write, what they want to pass on to others, or what they need to find out about.

I have seen writers who were best motivated in the middle of a crowded place like a coffee shop, pub, or restaurant; or writers who were quite the opposite, and preferred the quiet of home behind closed doors, even writers who used discussions with other people, or through verbal confrontations to motivate their writing.

All this reflects on different personalities and the needs they have to help their minds focus. A person might also be distracted through isolation yet at the same time have a desire to be creative, or ambitious because of a variety of reasons.

Encouragement to become motivated can come also from events external to the writer. For instance, a day starts beautifully, it is sunny, you feel positive about the day and then you feel moved to write. Motivation can happen by accident, the nature of motivation can vary according to the impact on the writer.

In the case of personal fear, motivation can move to become a form of defence, whereas contentment can result in a more independent motivation. There are many trigger mechanisms that can influence a writer's motivation.

We should however make the effort to remain positive, when we intend to write. Otherwise our writing will risk simply reflecting on the negative sides of life, which a reader can hardly honour. Motivation for writing needs to be carefully selected, because the power of a writer's words will impact on a reader significantly.

Now, what about the process of writing? This is, what is written, for what reason and how it is done. Newspapers, instructions, correspondence, books, legislation, jurisdiction, warnings, and research are to mention only a few. They all can differ in style, content, and last but not the least, whether they serve the purpose of not.

The use of technology in the process of writing, in today's world, has opened new windows of opportunity. We are now more efficient in our writing outcomes. What hasn't changed overtime is the need for good writing. This is where the 'talent' of writing comes in. We can learn to write correctly, but good writing also depends on the personality of the writer, and how well they express themselves.

Personality emerges from life experiences. With more experiences, you can possibly but not necessarily store more knowledge for the brain to recall. Every individual has the capacity to take experiences on board, to a greater or lesser degree.

Reading can be a substitute for personal experiences; it can help to learn from other people. This however should not prevent the individual from going out into the world and experiencing life and making their own experiences. A balance between reading and personal experiences serves a writer well.

How is good writing done? Sometimes when writing, we can find ourselves sitting in front of an empty page or a blank computer screen. At this point always remember, something good is never easy to come by, and by only trying, can the 'talent' emerge.

A few notes, a few words, and surprisingly the writing will slowly happen. It is predominantly the timing which will bring specific words and ideas out. Therefore, handle your brain gently and allow it to cooperate with you. Also, do not forget to let your brain recuperate after work, without losing the writing thread that you were following.

A time for good writing is determined by the alertness of the brain. Good writing doesn't mean copying other written sources - don't try to be a 'copycat'. The writer's personality should shine through the words, and this will determine the interest of the reader.

As previously mentioned life experiences are essential components of good writing. As soon as you feel you have learnt enough about writing correctly, nothing should stop you from writing and developing further good writing skills by simply practising writing. The more we write, the more variations we bring into our writing and this will help our personal writing style to emerge.

While writing, you should never forget to remain open to criticism; it's the touchstone of how serious a writer is towards his writing ideas and expression. To avoid criticism is a sign of writer insecurity; the hurdle of criticism is an essential part of achieving success.

From a personal perspective, I can tell you, life has kept me so busy, that it was only after leaving the professional 'tread mill' of work, at the age of 65 in 2006 that I found time to write.

The message is: It's never too late to start something new in life, including writing, and enjoying it.

* * * *

In addition: A little bit about me, the author Martin Kari.

I was born in 1941 in a very small country village of Transylvania, in the north of Romania. I was the second son of a long-standing farming family, and against all odds I survived the Second World War. During the war with Germany, I was fostered out, and these step-parents gave me, wanted or not, a direction in life.

Schools attempted to make a 'good' human being out of me. My time at the Music Conservatorium was supposed to give me a musical education. However, performing there was cut short, because my foster parents insisted they did not "want me to become a musician".

At that time, the words of parents were never disputed. So it was the 'school of life' with its ups and downs that directed me to what I am today. I left school to learn the trade of a toolmaker. 'Real life' told me, however, to do more in order to better myself. Engineering Studies and Matriculation was completed at evening school, and then entry to the venerable University 'Ruperto Carola' of Heidelberg from 1965 to 1968. Here I studied Sports, Medicine and Philology only to become disrupted by serious terror of the 'Baader-Meinhoff Group'.

My first excursions within Europe were with the Boy Scouts, and then through athletics. Because music was a hobby, it too helped me meet interesting people. One of these was 'Arja' from Finland, who became the most important person in my life. Finally I returned to my technical background, and together with Arja as my wife, overtime we created a family of three boys and three girls.

Professional appointments on four continents with my family, plus visits and excursions to many countries, gave opportunities to learn other languages as well. In 1981, the Australian Government brought us to Australia, where we established a successful foothold to our future.

Loyal to the principle, in life it is never too late to start something new, I started writing in 2006 at the age of 65, and I have enjoyed this activity ever since.

Chapter 13

JOY OF WRITING

(poem, Martin Kari)

Leave the daily rush aside,
Sit down and take your mind
On a journey of wishes and worries,
This is the joy of written words.
Thoughts, the first efforts
Towards wishes and worries,
They cross all borders
Like birds in the air.
They can rest on paper,
Or take a journey further,
To meet a few close-people first,
Eventually go out far
To many like-minded people.
But different-minded people , too.
Then time and coincidences
Will catch up with us again,
Feeding back good and less good answers
To our wishes and worries.
The price we have won, is joy.

Chapter 14

ONE SCHOOL DAY ONLY

In the early 1950's, school buses did not exist, and few parents could give children a lift to school. Therefore, as a child one had to get out of bed so much earlier to make the walk to school, to be there before the start of a school day at eight o'clock sharp.

A rainy day was never welcome, as it hindered the walk to school. Only a backpack was allowed, not a hand held bag. Usually I was joined by a school-mate during the walk to school, which took us along the river banks. We would see who could spot a fish in the water, first. It was tempting indeed to take time to watch the rainbow trout jump out of the shallow water.

The nearby church bell used to ring on every half an hour. The half-past-seven call was a reminder to not forget about school. However, on a sunny day, at least one more try skimming a flat stone from the riverbank was almost a must.

Ten minutes before the school day started the school bell would ring for the first time. By the time of the second ring, all students needed to be in their classrooms.

Care teachers usually watched for late arrivals, from the floor to ceiling windows. If you weren't a familiar face, you would be asked for your name and the reason for your lateness. Three notes around lateness resulted in a written report to your parents. After the second bell, it was expected that all students would be in their seats, in their classroom. Soon after this, the teachers would arrive.

Depending on the teacher, lessons could start straight away, or not. Already in the fifties, there were teachers who maintained discipline and teachers who struggled to achieve discipline. It was not necessarily the poor learners who created problems but the brighter ones.

Classrooms were also located in the basement of the two-storey schools. Almost regularly, during Art lessons in one of these basement classrooms, some students would manage to leave class undetected through the back window. A tennis court was only a few minutes walking distance away. It wasn't used for this purpose however. The tennis court was transformed into a soccer field, full of action packed fun. Taking care not to forget time, everybody usually could return to the class, without worry.

Once, though, the windows were all closed in the classroom. Someone must have found out about the escape. As a result, everybody had to stay inside during the break. The teacher pulled his cane out of the drawer. Each of the culprits had to stretch out his hand in front of the teacher, and receive a number of hits on his hand.

The teacher also had a surprise. The cane had been tampered with – cut all around. The moment the cane hit the first hand, bits and pieces of cane flew in all directions. The teacher looked at the remnants of the cane and said: "Well if you don't want your case settled with the cane, I can give you extra time after school to think about your pranks."

Bell ringing also announced changes of lesson. This time it was for music. For some students music was fun time. The teacher had to call for silence a number of times to remind all he was present. Once music theory was over, and when the teacher wasn't being interrupted by the 'stupidity' of the class, either a recorded piece of music would be presented, or the teacher would play some 'better music' on the piano.

For some reason, our teacher was happy one day, and twenty minutes before the end of music lesson he played on the piano. After that, he even presented a piece of recorded music. 'Bolero' by Ravel filled the air.

The teacher knew how to appreciate such a superior work. He stood next to his grand piano. He lifted himself up on to his toes, whilst supporting himself with his other hand on the piano. The teacher could only hold this position for a few minutes, before he needed to turn his head to catch what other sounds were in the air. His finger moved quickly to the stop button on the recorder. A whistle now reached the teacher; his face went purple with blood pressure. He couldn't hold back his disappointment.

"If you cannot listen, you are not worth a penny. Your whistle is disgusting. No more music from either the recorder or myself, until you have learnt to behave decently. Everybody shut up now. It's only me who will speak from now on!"

No school lesson was the same. Sixty years ago as for today, there were teachers who also had hardly any difficulties in managing a class. In these classes, the students of that time, and the students of today, usually found out quickly where they stood with the teacher.

One teacher of French found it appropriate to ask for outside help, when she thought she couldn't manage the class any longer. "I am leaving this class right now, and will not return until everybody behaves!" The noise in the class didn't stop, and the teacher didn't return.

When she did finally return, she came with the Principal, and he spoke to the class.

"All of you are to stop behaving disorderly, right now, and listen to what your teacher wants to teach you. I do not want to hear one single complaint any more, after I have left this class. Do I make myself understood? I leave you now with your French teacher. It's up to you whether you want to learn something." The lesson continued with authority, but with very little respect from the class.

The following Maths lesson shows how a teacher can build respect. A freshly baked teacher from the university started a Maths lesson for an exclusively female class. When the good looking young teacher entered the classroom, the girls showed that they were determined to test the teacher. Everybody kept talking as if the teacher was not present. They made no move to sit down. The teacher, who was also a teacher of Sports, was also very fit. He stood in front of the class, saying nothing, merely watching the circus going on. After a few minutes, without any change in the girls' behaviour he decided to act. Slowly, but carefully he rolled up both his shirt sleeves, one by one, showing his muscles. Then he added the following words. "If you can't behave properly, you will have to put up with my muscles."

"Wow!" was the unanimous response from the students. Every student moved without delay to her place, and teaching could begin.

A teacher of English however managed his lessons in a different way. Although not teaching music, he occasionally brought his guitar along to his English class. Students of that time loved English songs. What a difference music can make when learning a language. Everybody in class, without exception, wanted to learn the English language through this easy backdoor of music. Some students even started their own bands through this experience, and competition developed amongst them.

The fun of music had to serve of course the bigger goal of learning English. To achieve this, the teacher made it clear that songs would only be played when the necessary learning had also progressed. The 'carrot' of the music has always worked from times past to now.

One more prank during the day is worth noting. The next lesson was Biology. Slides were being shown, and as a result the blinds had to be shut in order to keep the daylight out. The teacher kept pointing on the screen with a stick to underline his words. Later when the teacher detected a noise unrelated to his teaching, he suddenly switched, the lights on in the room, stating "if you think you can either fall asleep or try to disrupt my lesson with nonsense, I'll stop the next time and we will have a written test, so you can show what you have learned. John, you had better wake up! You, Marc and Linda, as well. If you keep talking you can go out and stay out. I'm talking now while you shut up and listen!"

Despite this, another disturbance took place, so the teacher had to raise his voice again. "Why is the door in the back not closed? We can't have light from the outside because of the projector." Nothing happened, and therefore the teacher's voice went up a few more notches. "As you are already on your feet Lisa, hurry and close the door for us." Lisa stuttered without moving from her spot. 'Bu…..b…..but Mister…….'

"I don't want to listen to anything you have to say. Do as you are told! How long do you want me to wait? This group of students is annoying me. I will switch on the lights and see for myself what is going on."

The lights on, the teacher became flabbergasted, when he realized what really had taken place in the classroom. Lisa's mother had tried to leave a message for Lisa at the half-open back door.

"Lisa, why didn't you tell me about your mother being here? Please, excuse my words we will sort this out quickly so that we can return to our lesson. Mrs Greenwood, please don't hold this incident against me. We all know how difficult it can be sometimes to teach the younger generation."

At the end of this school day, an excursion into the nearby forest with the Biology teacher was still on. Just after the whole class had reached the foot path, led by the teacher, two upset crossing-sweepers appeared. They pointed straight towards the student called Martin, indicating to the teacher that he had called them ugly names. The teacher did not hesitate, but turned towards Martin and gave him a proper hiding in front of everyone. In his rage, the teacher added, "Now we will go back to school and have a real written test, not in Biology but in Maths. You can all thank Martin for that!"

Nobody was happy but the maths test took place. Early the next day, it became clear that what the crossing-sweepers had claimed was unfounded. In the next Biology lesson, the teacher stated in front of the class, "Martin, I'm sorry about what has happened. All I can say to you is that you have completed by far the best maths test, congratulations, and as for the bashing, I owe you an apology. You now have one bashing in credit for the future," and that was that.

After lessons, all students left school, with the exception of those who had received a detention. They were advised to complete their detention, and not make it worse for themselves by staying away. According to a mutual agreement between parents and school, students were to go straight home without delay. It was, however, still tempting to catch trout by hand along the riverbanks on the way home. When this happened, big trouble would be already brewing at home. House arrest would be hanging in the balance between school and home.

Pranks aside, school and parents were both serious about education, even then. The next generation would not be able to follow successfully in the steps of their forefathers, without school achievement. However, sixty years ago, nothing was so bad that it could not be overcome.

Everything seems to repeat itself throughout history. Therefore, a younger generation could, and still can, have a successful education. In the end though, life is and as it always has been, our best teacher.

One last note, the pranks described here are out of the 'real' world and did indeed take place, albeit sixty years ago.

Chapter 15

FIRE

𝓕ire is final, yes and no! It burns down everything, but it can create new growth in its aftermath. This contrast of destruction and bringer of life is the life cycle of nature. As such it must be regarded as controversial.

Where do we find the source of this controversy? We are standing right on it, on our fireball of Earth.

Australia in particular, in its isolation from the rest of the world, displays the evolution of fire survival, and the challenges of fire versus the creation of new life.

It is also said nothing is totally bad even after fire, as long as hope survives.

Chapter 16

SOMETHING ANNOYS ME

Why should something annoy me? This question arises, when for the most part our daily life runs on an even keel. For this to always be the case is however wishful thinking. The reality is that rivalry between our 'likes' and 'dislikes' keeps us in the realm of being annoyed. We will all experience being annoyed to varying degrees, from time to time.

Here is a typical example:

After a long working week, it is the weekend. On Friday night of this weekend, Jim gives his mate Robert a call to remind him that on the next day, Saturday afternoon, they have both planned to go to the movies with their girlfriends. "Be there at least half an hour earlier, so that we can enjoy a refreshing ice-cream at the local coffee shop," Jim organises. "Instead of taking two cars, and dealing with the inevitable parking problems, can you pick me up at my place?" Jim asks. "We can then drive to your Jackie's place and my Nicole's. I'll give you some petrol money before we get to the ladies. Make sure you're at my place by one o'clock sharp. I am so looking forward to our outing."

Everything is organised, and all that remains is for everyone to stay with the plans.

One o'clock Saturday arrives, but that is all. Jim watches the clock, and then decides to phone Robert, but with no luck. He is really annoyed, and wonders to himself, who can you rely on in today's world.

He thought they had reached an agreement about the plans for today. Jim decides to take matters into his own hands, drive his own car, and collect Nicole for the movie outing. He will see if Robert and Jackie turn up. He realizes he'd better quickly call Nicole to explain why he's late.

At the cinema however, only a few minutes after Jim and Nicole's arrival, who should turn up? Robert with Jackie! At first, Jim pretends not to see them. However, Robert shouts out to Jim, "good to see you have made it."

Jim replies, "Is that all you have to say? I thought we agreed on a plan yesterday? You must be as mindless as a chicken, or Jackie has influenced you. You really have annoyed me. Firstly you don't arrive at my place at all; secondly, you pretend everything is all right. It might be for you, but not for me. So that there isn't a third time maybe we should try to forget about what has already happened, and enjoy the afternoon at the movies."

The moral of the story is: the more preparation undertaken, the easier for annoyances to occur when things go wrong.

It doesn't always need to be an entire story behind our annoyances. Let's look at some small incidents which make up our daily lives.

I rush in the morning to make the city bus station only to find that the bus drivers are all on strike. This annoys me, because I do not know how I am going to get to work.

With the shopping done, the goods are all in the trolley, ready for the checkout. The goods are scanned, and the total cost is displayed on the screen. I am asked how I would like to pay by the 'checkout chick'. I suddenly realize that I have no wallet. My wallet is probably still waiting at home for me. This event does not only annoy me.

John is running around like a headless chicken, wondering what he has done with his glasses. He asks his wife Ann if she has seen them. Ann calms John down, and asks him, "What have you got sitting on your nose?" John realizes he's done it again, it must be his age, cutting short not only his eye sight, but also his memory. Ann has saved his day.

Now, here's something that shouldn't annoy any of us, that is the monthly homework of our writers' group. This chapter is just such a piece. Why? First of all, my understanding is that we are free to participate or not, and secondly, it is a good writing discipline to contribute something to the meeting and not simply go to the meetings and expect others to do the work of keeping the interest in our writers group alive. It's exactly at this point of commitment where some other writers' groups fall short, and wonder why members turn away. If we want to improve in our writing, we can learn from every little bit of writing, including all the pieces that every member can offer.

Do we have to become annoyed? As humans, we cannot avoid being annoyed from time to time; we are not perfect. As long as our gall bladder doesn't tell us it has had enough, we can stay on track with the good sides of life. Life however, will be much better, when we manage to reduce our annoyance level. One thing we can do to keep the annoyance level in check, is to take nothing too seriously, and to never expect our fellow humans to do what we expect them to do.

Disappointments are the starting point of becoming annoyed. It has taken me so far, seventy years of my life to cut back on becoming unnecessarily annoyed and still I'm not sure whether I have mastered all the learnings. The main thing is that we all stay on that road working to keep our annoyance level in check.

Chapter 17

FUN

On the one hand 'fun' can have a wide range of meanings, but not on the other hand when it comes down to what is the reality of fun.

So just what is 'fun'?

In a few words, fun is the result of personal effort – no effort, no fun!

And how do we show this?

At the staging of a recent Brisbane Show if you were to have visited the show in order to have fun, without spending any money, you would have been left with an unpleasant truth: efforts using hindsight change the nature of fun, whereas prior efforts help support fun.

It is no wonder that the original meaning of fun embraces cheating, hoaxing and fooling.

A hint for meaningful writing:

> *Words are something we should not waste, they should come out of deep prior reflection.*

Chapter 18

THE ART OF WRITING, ITS RULES AND REALITIES

"A battle of words is always a win"
Goethe

"People can be taught to write if the literacy gift is not there," is a quote from <u>A Fence Around the Cuckoo</u> by Ruth Park.

What are our aims with writing: to entertain, to inform, to gossip or to climb the heights of literature?

Writing could be seen as the next step up from verbal communication, because it makes the words said, visible. Like everything else in life, it starts out small and imperfect. One thing that helps though, even in the early stages of writing, is without doubt, reading.

Reading however, can help the writer only when he/she actually becomes active. A great many steps need to be followed in order to achieve writing success.

I remember for instance, at an early age (when school had taught me sufficiently about 'correct writing') that mum would remind me, now and then, to write a letter to grandpa before going out to play with school mates. This might sound trivial, but let's ask the question: how many youngsters can confidently write a letter today?

It is the discipline behind everything that often determines where our efforts will lead us. Isn't it also true, in writing, that the 'early bird catches the worm'? What about rules? Are they there to be bent or ignored? How strictly do the rules of writing apply to writing? During our school lessons, we are taught that writing starts with the preparation of thoughts, and a list of contents. How often do we write something, though, just by 'fiddling' around with our thoughts and the required content list comes about either during the writing exercise or even at the end of it?

A finished script doesn't tell about the way it came together. One learning out of this would be: write, and while you are writing know that you are also thinking more productively, because you are visualizing your thoughts with words. This becomes an additional awareness. By following such a rule, the most important ingredient for writing becomes obvious. This is fantasy. No fantasy, no real writing!

Rules have their limitations. The general rules for writing that are given to us establish only our guidelines for writing. The better writer also develops his/her own rules through their reading. Rules such as: keep writing, make use of critical awareness and maintain patience, together with stamina. The writer who has already been published is the one who best understands what all this means.

A writer's self-reflection on their writing is as essential to their work, as are real-life experiences, a down to earth imagination and the ability to make comparisons. Let us not confuse the issue with too many words, as these are the 'underdogs' of the central theme. Simplicity in writing is the ultimate goal. We all know that we are good at making things difficult. It is only with time, after our first attempts that we discover simplicity with our words.

Searching for words in comprehensive dictionaries can often divert understanding from the central theme, often confusing the reader. Isn't the reader, the writer's judge? What does a reader expect from the writer? Surely what is required is true and honest writing.

Today there is too much 'fashionable' information around on writing. More than ever, a writer needs to maintain their courage to maintain his/her own writing style. Thus writing is on the way to becoming an art form. Art being classified as an individual's expression offered to others, whereby the artist/writer creates something that can communicate collectively.

What makes the difference between a speaker and a writer? I believe that speaking out asks for at least one preceded thought, whereas with writing, the more thoughts and structure that go into it, the better the writer emerges. That is why, in most cases, a good speech is prepared initially in written form.

The art of writing can find itself at home in many formats. Let me just mention a few: novels, poetry, varieties of stories, reports, biographies, fiction, non-fiction, mystery, romance, adventure.

Most forms of writing have their own established structure. It is there that some rules apply. Having a supply of all-round-knowledge can only be helpful in co-existence with a writer's skill and creativity. Balance is again the key for a writer; we can engage in learning about writing and neglect our writing creativity. Real learning means preparing one's own individual activity. This is what makes or breaks a writer's success.

Something not to be underestimated is the economics of writing. All writing can sell. Publishing initiatives such as: the Internet, digital books and self-publishing are just to name a few options. Quality writing is produced today mainly by a team of authors, editors and people capable of independent, constructive criticism. Publishers focus increasingly on the economic side of the publishing business.

To summarize, so far, what makes writing an art, there are endless possibilities of formats for written dialogues, and collecting ideas. There is a range of stylistic features that give the thrill of both figurative and symbolic use of language. The writer can modulate his/her expression from a cry, to a sigh; from laughter to regret, to a curse and much more.

Everything written is unique because every moment can unleash from the brain a different spark, never to be reproduced. This turns all creativity into an accidental, timely dependency. In simple words, what we write today, we would write differently tomorrow if we stayed creative, and did not become a copy-cat.

Rules and realities are writing pressures, which the writer must balance if wanting to be heard. Balance is everything. Who will become a renowned writer? What some publishers practise today is often at loggerheads with what a writer is attempting to achieve. Publishers too are driven by market demands.

The major discrepancy between writing to the rules, and the reality of acceptance, is that only a few names make it. It is more the work of a writer that will make him/her famous. It is not the rules, or the publicity stunt, or a title, or a name which will build a writer's lasting success. The art of writing is to connect as many readers as possible to a writer's work. This cuts across whole societies, regardless of a person's standing in society. Keeping this in mind, it is surely true that we all could somehow succeed in writing if only we persist long enough in pursuing such a goal.

Some writing may lay claim to be 'good' writing if not 'artistic' writing. What makes art of some words? Often it is the symbolic and metaphorical (vivid, figurative) elements that enhance writing. Some points to consider with regards to the topic "The Art of Writing, its rules and realities", are as follows:

a) There are many ups and downs, like the ebb and flow of the sea. (Emile Carles)
b) The purple trumpets spilled over the side of the fence; it was as though we had a whole backyard filled with purple flowers. A

sort of hallelujah chorus of blooms trumpeting away as hard as they could to welcome us to our first home. (Bryce Courtney)

c) The whole world marches to the tune of sobs and sighs. (Bryce Courtney)

d) I'm not as smart as most, but I work harder, because I am from the school of hard knocks. (R.M.Williams)

e) But, like a mature wine, it gets better and more interesting as one awakens old memories and brings forth that which is significant in one's life and perhaps pass over that which is not. (Bryce Courtney)

f) Doing things, not having things, is the whole point of life. The joy must come from what we do, not from what we do with the money we make from what we do. (R.M.Williams)

g) One other but very important reason for wanting to write is to leave a legacy for descendants so that they may learn and understand from whence we came and the kind of conditions under which we grew up in the years that followed. (Bryce Courtney)

h) I do measure a man by the means he uses to climb the ladder of success; success has to be a journey and not a destination. (R.M.Williams)

Chapter 19

THE WHEEL BARROW

Let's give a voice to the wheel barrow, too,
with a limit of 100 words only.

The wheel on its own cannot do much
And so cannot the barrow.
To be true to its origin, the barrow needs
A bear behind it to make a wheel working.
And the ones using the wheel barrow
Know only too well what wonderful tool
It can be around a house,
In a garden, building a house.
It takes and moves everything
That fits into its barrow :
Leaves, branches, soil, sand, stones, cement,
Mortar, bricks, timber, tiles
And even joins the fun
To eventually wheel a child
In lieu of a pram
Which all depends
On the person's bear-skills.

(Words, Martin Kari, 2015)

Chapter 20

A BOOK AND ITS JOURNEY

It gives me great pleasure to speak tonight to this audience at the new 'Hub-Library' at Caboolture. Thank you for joining me in a discussion of the topic <u>A Book and its Journey</u>. My name is Martin Kari, and I have lived in this local community for 25 years.

*W*riting a book and having it published is a special experience and achievement. Certainly I am not alone in writing. To date I've published 7 books, all since I retired from the professional treadmill, at the age of 65 years. What has been an important message for me is that it's never too late to start something new in life.

Before continuing to speak, I might ask my audience what questions they already have, so that we might create an even wider, more open discussion. Alternatively, we could save the questions to the end. I give you the choice.

You will be encouraged throughout my presentation to come forward with questions for later on. Instead of speaking only about my dealings with the publishing industry, I thought it would be useful to give some information on the theme of my talk, 'A book and its journey'. Some information might be new to some of you.

Wanting to write is the starting point, but then we have to proceed to the action. I found out very quickly that writing, in particular 'good writing' is not easy. You need to have a good idea, and then avoid becoming a copy-cat. The emphasis here is on two things, civil courage and knowledge. The best knowledge comes from personal experience.

To bring the words to paper, either empty page or computer screen is a challenge from the start. A pencil or pen is not in demand anymore. It took me quite some time to change to keyboard writing on a computer. I discovered that writing first by hand, and then transferring it to the computer was too time consuming. Everything in today's world must be word processed.

It is also highly unlikely that a first attempt at writing will succeed. So much editing, and redrafting will improve the product, and you become a better writer. Better writing is generally, the use of words involving both figurative language and formed comparisons. One example of this can be seen in the writing of the late Australian author, Bryce Courtenay who refers to open-door-writing: "the purple trumpets spilled over the side of the fence; it was as though we had a whole backyard filled with purple flowers. A sort of hallelujah chorus of blooms trumpeting away as hard as they could to welcome us to our first home."

Closed-door-writing would seem more like, "the first time we arrived in our new home through the garden." It is just stating the facts, and there is no further invitation to the reader to form a picture, or to interact with the text.

Now, let's suppose we have completed that hurdle of writing, and we are happy with the result. It has been self-checked, and there appears to be no more need for refinement. The 'file' is saved both to the computer, and also to a memory stick, and perhaps additionally to a 'C.D.' and an external hard drive. What is the next step with a written file as we aim for publication?

A common next step is with an editor, or through a publisher contact, he/she finds an editor. The writer may even choose to not deal with a professional editor when considering other avenues to publication.

Firstly, let us look at the traditional avenue to book publication through a Publishing House.

Either the editor of your choice, or one of the publisher's, with some luck, will add the manuscript of an 'unknown' author on to a pile in order to receive an opinion on the quality of the writing. In many cases it will be a case of "if you don't hear back from us, your manuscript has not been successful." The writer's chosen editor is more likely to look at your manuscript. Publishing Houses claim to have piles of manuscripts in front of them for evaluation.

How can a keen writer win such a battle? The answer is, shop around! The same patience and time spent on preparing the manuscript, is also required at the publishing stage.

When the 'bell of entrance' rings to the publishing game, luck will have played its role. As soon as editing takes place, the manuscript receives corrections and side-notes, which a writer is asked in a forward and return process. How far opinions differ here, about changes to be made, is a matter of diplomacy. If you want to succeed, you follow the rules given to you. It remains to be seen how much of a discussion about the manuscript occurs, when it is accepted by the publisher.

As soon as editing has taken place, the writer's foot is in the door for further developments, unless the manuscript is not deemed commercial in the market of the publisher. Driven by their market, publishers have a liking of their own. A written contract from the publisher should bring more certainty on a book's journey.

A publishing contract is however a legal document which requires careful attention from the writer. It is usually a reason for a celebration, but let 'caution be the mother of all wisdom'.

It can only help an author to make sure that they fully understand a publishing contract; if in doubt, seek advice. Six months of 'polishing' a manuscript appears realistic, do not expect a rush. Unless you are in the eyes of a publisher a 'genius' it will take time.

After the editing has gone forwards and backwards, satisfying the varying parties, the race for publication is still on. The next steps are: formatting of the book, the publisher's imprint with ISBN number, and the book design. The importance of a book title cannot underestimated.

Often a right title can make or break the success of a book. An ISBN number confirms the book as a new title, and does not already exist. Depending on the publisher, an input of ideas from the author will be considered.

From here on, the book journey is mainly in the hands of the publisher. For a lengthy time period, an author might not hear anything from the publisher An air of expectation will be hanging around. Sometimes, the author lives with their doubts, an unexpected breakthrough will occur, and a first proof-print will happen. The author must ensure that this is the book they want the reading world to receive. From this point, there is no return. The book is now on the road of hope, destination success.

How many books are printed with a first edition is an economical consideration by the publisher. Most of the time books will arrive in book shops, through the distribution network. This avoids the 'bottle-neck' situation of self-publishers, which I well explain later.

Books selling in shops need a business structure in place, with accounts established. Selling books means business, and it is rare that authors will have established accounts with book outlets.

One exemption to this has become the Online Sales area, or Amazon. Not only publishers, but all individual self-publishers can deal through the internet with these selling points. A tug of war between traditional publishing houses and the growing number of alternative publishing pathways takes place here. It is up to an author to choose the best pathway for him/herself. Everyone needs to be mindful that publishing is always changing. To hold firm to traditional pathways can provide sureness, but it can also be short-sighted and miss other opportunities.

Let's return to the traditional publishing pathway. The 'proof-print' has made its appearance, and now the author might be asked for some personal details, including suitable photo-material so that publicity can be prepared. In some cases, reviews of the book are used to raise awareness for the publisher, and for inclusion on the book. Depending on the importance of the book's journey, the press media might add its influence with an article or a publicity note. Author's readings at special venues, bookshops, libraries and special events can also be organised.

Hopefully, this information isn't too off-putting for the author, as there is still much more to the publishing journey. Let's not become disillusioned by the difficulties, the serious author cannot avoid the journey, if they want to pursue maximum publishing potential. Some might like the easy going approach, others will take the challenge head on, while there are those who will remain contented with what they have written. Each approach will determine the course of the book's journey and its destination.

A first edition is a hurdle; more following editions of the book will open the door more widely to success. Staying with supporting measures for book promotion remains essential. The question arises here, who is behind all this? Can the author deal with book promotion without losing his/her writing track? One answer to this stays with the publisher. They have the business of book promotion and sale in place. However, nothing is free. That is why charges apply, particularly in today's profit-driven world. Only the renowned author will experience exemption.

No matter how a book starts off, the author has reason to celebrate. Listings of the book with local libraries, regional libraries, and the National library lead to lending rights which remunerate the author with one dollar for each book lending. (still in 2015). If an author is particularly diverse, they might present the book in another language either with their own skill or through a translator of the publishing house. NOTE A book should never be translated word for word, as this is how an originally good book can become an inferior one. A book in another language has to be newly written, preferably by the author, with regard for the idioms of the destination language.

As previously mentioned, there are other ways of having a book produced, as in self-publishing. In this area, everything is left to the author to control, and to organise. If editing of the manuscript is required, an editor of the author's choice is given the task; further on, printing, keeping stock, marketing, selling, listing, advertising the book, and last but not least, paying for all the expenses.

But this is not all bad news! On the contrary, the competent author can have with self-publishing not only all the work, but the benefits too. Authors who are flexible, hard-working, and lucky will reach a higher step on the success-ladder. How long this success will last, will depend also on the circumstances surrounding the book's journey, which are beyond the influence of the individual author.

Success comes from outside. With or without a publisher, all an author can do is prepare for success, by hard work.

Chapter 21

CAN 'DUGONG' STAND FOR CABOOLTURE?

'Dugong' (Dujong) is a Malay name for the sea cow which belongs to the classification of hoofed animals. This animal is found mainly in the sea waters of the Red Sea, the Indian Ocean, as well as Moreton Bay, on the East Coast of Australia, near the Queensland capital of Brisbane.

Whether the dugong left the land and adapted to the sea, or has never left the sea, is not yet clearly established. Its cylindrical smooth body is propelled in shallow sea water by a horizontal pair of flippers in place of two hind-legs, while the front legs are transformed into two rounded shorter 'fins'.

Like its family 'cow' on a green meadow, this 'sea cow' too grazes on the green meadow; only it is a green meadow of sea algae and sea grasses on the sea bed, which are within reach of the sunlight required to allow vegetation to flourish. A thick upper lip moves in bristled side-folds enabling it to feed on the sea vegetation. The dugong has no teeth.

Its compact cylindrical appearance, fair colour and skilled moves in the ocean are attributed to its 'celestial-creation' as depicted in the early cultures of Egypt, the Indian and Indonesian religions, and the mythology of the Northern Australian Aborigine.

The dugong is a protected species, with only indigenous Australians exempted to hunt it, as part of their traditional culture.

To understand the special features of a dugong, one must venture by boat onto the waters of Moreton Bay, selecting a calm, sunny day, with plenty of time available. It is especially in the early hours of a sunny day when the dugong can be found feeding on the ocean vegetation near the coast.

In the latter part of the day, dugongs seek the protection of deeper water. If undisturbed, the dugong will move its stout body slowly along the ocean floor. It is most often easily recognizable with its light colour against the deep dark blue of the ocean. It has been described as a bit like a cow swimming under the surface of the water. The name of 'sea cow' is a product of this observation.

Dugongs are by nature curious, but careful enough to avoid proximity too close to humans. This is a different behaviour to that of dolphins, which often seek out the company of humans. Compared with the dolphin, a dugong is less capable of a fast disappearance from its main predator, the shark. The dugong's behaviour is more that of a wise creature using caution as a life practice.

It is from here, that the dugong has attracted wisdom as its trademark. As we have for many other species on Earth, our species highly endangers the existence of dugongs. Their numbers have recently dwindled not only from hunting, but more so from the pollution of oceans which results also in a decimation of their natural feeding grounds.

What the frog can tell us about the health of the land environment, the same can be said of the dugong in its maritime environment. It tells us about ocean health. No dugong will mean for us, that we will receive few messages of the sea or its health.

Now to answer the question: Can the dugong represent Caboolture as its totem? I very much doubt this, as the spread of dugong is wider than the area of Caboolture, with the largest dugong population to be found in Australia, actually located at Shark Bay in the Indian Ocean, off Western Australia

Dugong feeding in the sea

Chapter 22

HOMELESSNESS

We are all migrants in Australia, having arrived from somewhere else in the world. A lot of the population can still remember what Australia was like when they arrived. Twenty-eight years ago, when my family and I migrated to Australia after living and working in three other continents, Australia had a lot to offer. House prices in Brisbane were most affordable; qualified, permanent work was available, and health care was readily accessible.

Homelessness was not spoken about, nor were the issues of health care or education as prominent as they became in 2010. What caused Australia to move away from this lucky country position?

Too much foreign interest has dominated Australia, leaving the country's resident populace out of focus. International interest has become a priority, and today we talk of increasing the population, as politicians tell us this is the way out of our current impasses. How could increasing the population help fix the current infrastructure problems when the latest population increases are said to be responsible for so many shortcomings?

Today we should be aware of the burdens we pass on to future generations. There has been a shift away from job security, as well as inflated house prices in order to satisfy financial markets, the unhealthy financial state of the country, along with decreases in discipline, beliefs, and a decline in personal values of friendship, family, and community combined with increasing pressures on the natural environment.

If we continue to push these 'inconveniences' under the carpet, and just 'talk the talk' without much concern about 'walking the walk', we risk becoming 'ostriches' with our heads in the sand, and miss not seeing the imminent danger of the consequences.

It is important to remember that those who do not like constructive questioning, and the answers to these questions, do not want progress. As I am advocating progress, I will keep writing. However, whether ostrich or not, the dangers will not go away on their own. We need to be prepared to face what we have created.

One of the issues to be faced has become homelessness. What has created this? Homelessness is one outcome of our time, which is linked to many causes. Some of these causes and effects can seem difficult to recognise.

Everything in life starts small, and can develop over time, without due attention, into something difficult to control. Most of the time, when something has turned bad enough, it is only then that the public gets a wake-up-call. This is then the moment that politics enters the discussion to point-score for political advantage. Thus, the outcomes are politically motivated, expensive and often unhelpful.

More helpful are public driven initiatives that prepare step by step solutions. These, in cooperation with political forces, can lead to down-to-earth, practical solutions which are workable. This is the idea of community participation, with a variety of people bringing together their divers opinions, aiming to reach conclusions decided on by the majority.

What can a writer contribute to the urgent discussion of homelessness? I believe, we need to go back to our origins to understand where we have all come from.

A. INTERNAL CAUSES FOR HOMELESSNESS

1. FAMILY – All life starts from this point. Nature demands that young life is protected until fully developed. Family has primarily met this demand. Failure to deliver positive starting points at the level of family, has wide reaching consequences in the social development of an individual.

    Family is the first playground for youngsters where they learn lessons from mistakes. If this does not occur, then missed lessons lead to later life difficulties, or simply anti-social behaviour. The damage is done by exposing a vulnerable child to a hostile family environment. A life starting out in shambles is like picking up broken glass, which has the potential for further hurt.

    Family is the foundation of every society. Failure in recognising this appropriately or experimenting with new family models invariably leads into unpredictable territory. This can contribute to a situation of homelessness because of an early loss of home security.

    How to tackle family life in order that a positive contribution is made to each family member is essential. Every family has to work towards this goal according to their capabilities. For instance whether both parents work, or adopt the traditional model, of one working and one looking after the family household and the offspring in particular, has to be decided upon.

    In past times, other members of the extended family like an aunt, uncle, or grandparent often filled the gap of family supervision.

    In countries like Sweden, it has long been culturally established that the parent with the better income works outside the family home, and the other parent, whether husband or wife, looks after family affaires. Not only in Sweden, but in other Scandinavian countries such as Denmark, Norway and Finland, an income is provided for the house parent. However, this comes at the price of a very high taxation level for all incomes! This shows only that we cannot have something without paying for it in another way.

Governments are irresponsible in creating people who expect handouts, as the question remains unanswered, who is going to pay for it? Not everything that seems popular in the eyes of politicians is necessarily good. Sometimes, hard, uneasy decisions need to have priority over popular demand. This is where the mutual responsibilities of all parties and the common interests of all parties should be discussed, when dealing with homelessness.

2. EDUCATION – In a majority of cases, education features as the next step in an individual's development. A roof over your head is still an essential part of developing a future independent career in life. However, every individual has their own timetable for maturity. Some mature earlier than others, some never seem to mature.

During difficult phases of development, both parents and teachers need to remain impartial. Let us not forget how we were. Problems in education cannot be ignored but should be dealt within the guide lines of discipline and respect, never forgetting to model what is expected. Any discrepancy between what is seen in adults and what is said to young people can open the well-known generation gap. This generation gap is a distancing in mutual understanding. It is not necessarily the 'naughty' student, but the misunderstood intellect behind it, which often derails not only adolescents but parents, teachers and everybody close by.

When adolescents are difficult to comprehend, this should be regarded as a challenge in which the adults have to show a direction, maintain discipline and not become the issue themselves. In a search for an identity, the adolescent seeks support not disapproval. Setting the course wrongly here has the potential to push the adolescent to seek recognition in other ways.

Parents and schools play an important part in the gradual move from home by providing protection as one journeys towards self-management in society. Controversy during this growing independence can lead to a trust deficit between the adolescent and the significant adults of parents and educators. It is understood that 'great oaks from little acorns grow', and the impact of disagreements leading to adolescent-rejection is the road towards homelessness.

3. INDEPENDENCE

Depending on how the ground has been prepared with the adolescent, the steps towards an individual life will stay connected to past experiences, Some might stand up to their own life's challenges, while others may lose confidence in their own ability to resist outside influences. Then a common ground with the past is lost.

Turning back the wheel of life events in order to identify contributors to emerging homelessness is complex. We are all socially connected to each other, and as such we all share responsibility for the impact of negative 'growing-up' events.

B. **EXTERNAL CAUSES FOR HOMELESSNESS**

1. NEGATIVE ENVIRONMENTS – Drugs, alcohol, crime and sex are discussed today as if everybody has been there, and can look back on it from a safe distance. The reality however is that such constant naïve discussion simply invites others to test drive the 'benefits'. Once on that pathway, personal willpower remains at constant loggerheads with other negative intentions. If the negative prevails, homelessness will become an outcome of an unstable life.

How unpredictably children can develop, is in part explained by the genes of our ancestors. Some traits become accidentally activated within us.

As part of my personal experience, my wife and I have raised three sons and three daughters, and we would watch how differently each one grew up. One daughter in particular tested us as parents, from the age of fourteen. School was boring, her parents were leading an ancient lifestyle, and instead of sleeping at night we were looking for the whereabouts of the daughter. Homelessness became the official explanation despite there being plenty of room on the family property. Officialdom even pushed the 'right' of the fourteen year old adolescent, declaring her free to make her own decisions.

"As a fourteen year old she can decide what she wants"; what a load of irresponsible rubbish! Since when are we master of our own life at fourteen years of age? The parents' insistence not to give in paid its dividends. Luckily other areas were tested without irreversible personal damage and the daughter eventually returned home. A home must be a family castle for all family members to return to. Our problem with one offspring, who regained her position at home, enabled the daughter to pursue success in her life.

Thus the family situation had become very close to an outcome of homelessness for an offspring. There is usually much behind the homeless scene than is easily recognized. We should not forget that young migrants too are particularly vulnerable, as they are drawn between their new society, and a search for identity reflecting their cultural origins.

Parents on the other hand usually maintain their tradition and culture, while the next generation is more likely disconnected from it, as they seek the life of their new surroundings. This in many cases causes disharmony with the parents.

Throughout much of history, families in the past lived in close communities, sharing close ties, and passing on cultural links. The multicultural society emerging nowadays is still in limbo with tradition. We can live without tradition cannot be an answer. More time will need to elapse for society to develop in a multicultural way that is beneficial to a majority of people. Only history will show whether this new society is positioned upwards or further down on the score board.

2. LIVING BEYOND MEANS

Financial over commitment, job-loss, parental divorce, serious sickness, accidents, death of significant people and gambling can all lead to homelessness. Usually it is the young, more than the old who bear the brunt of such developments.

Sudden changes can shake a family, particularly if precautionary measures have not been put in place to avert the impact of such events. Unfortunately, it must be said that it is often easier to fall into homelessness than to get out of it. Keeping this in mind, all efforts need to run to a cautious economy to avoid homelessness in the first place.

3. WAR, natural disaster and fire can also take a home away. Homelessness in bad times needs people to reenergize to rebuild. During good times at least social services can provide some safeguarding measures.

In recent years, social services have become essential for family shortcomings. The downside of this is that people can become reliant on someone else with some attempting to get as much as possible out of a service, where no responsibility is expected. This sends the wrong signal to the next generation, who may not understand that nothing in life is free. If a 'freebie' is however handed out, it should not be forgotten that somebody has to fit the bill.

Even so, when the bill cannot be met anymore, it leaves the accustomed 'beggar' high and dry for not knowing how to tackle a problem by breaking it down into more manageable smaller portions in order to work out steps on it. This is a case for then the 'talk show' turning into action, and is very much an issue related to homelessness.

C. REMEDIES FOR HOMELESSNESS

Homelessness cannot be resolved with a handout. It is far too complex an issue to be solved by one single measure. Firstly, we must acknowledge that an understanding of the issue must be nurtured, and acknowledging community-wide that we are all connected in the responsibility of homelessness, and that we have all contributed to it in a way, even if unwittingly.

Having established that there is no quick fix as the causes leading to homelessness are deeply rooted within communities. Long term planning is required, after a thorough diagnosis of the issue. Community representation from: parents, teachers, social and community representatives, politicians, police, industry, arts and sciences should all be heard in a solution-finding process.

From here, it is a step in the right direction to call upon a community initiative in preparing a plan. All should have their say on the matter so that a practical committee is then able to draw up an action plan. Such a community initiative should compel governing authorities to forward the plan to a realization of outcomes for such a burning issue.

Here is a summary of the steps:

1. Establish the homelessness nature of known citizens and further investigate
2. Prioritize homelessness characteristics: force majeure, capital bungle, homeless youth with/without parental home, adult/aged homelessness, past/present negligence to disadvantaged groups.

    Why prioritize? It is unfair to put all cases of homelessness in one pot, regardless of prioritized need. In establishing priorities, the ones in urgent need can receive earlier effective help before the whole task collapses.
3. Consideration has to also be given to a quick solution in achieving accommodation for people. Volunteer homes, public

facilities, providing incentives and scrutinizing safety issues are all part of the solutions.

4. Once the preceding steps have been undertaken it is easier to prioritize the housing solution required, and to estimate the financial commitment. However, here is the integral part; nothing should be free of obligation. An obligation should be linked to a home recipient as part of their contribution to the community solution. The best economical link would be 'work'. Work is a right, like a home, and therefore should become part of the solution, assisting both the community and the homeless.

5. The indigenous population in the Northern Territory need obligations linked to their social benefits. No commitment to basic education should mean no benefit receiving. This could also be extended to their community help. Work is a good therapy for all sorts of behaviour disorders, carrying the mind away from other dilemmas.

6. Community help needs to include a variety of supportive corrections, not just the provision of housing.

7. Throwing money at the problem of homelessness without engaging all persons will fail to address the long term solution required. Quick fixes don't help. We certainly have to become active by engaging private initiatives, religious organisations, social groups, volunteers, businesses, governments, banks – yes banks too if they want to maintain their self-declared community image. Incentives in the right area could work wonders for our fellow citizens.

EPILOGUE

History can show us a lot about housing issues. One is probably worth mentioning here because it highlights the dangers of mishandling the problem: In the nineteenth century the Russian General, Potjomkin, commissioned on behalf of Katharine 11 the Great, some housing projects in the Russian south. He also organised the Tsarina to inspect the project from a specially organised shipping cruise on the Volga. From the distance, the villages of the project could be seen with their colourful facades; however the money had found its way into corruption, leaving only the facades.

Today, Potjomkin Villages are still around. Governments in many parts of the world have built whole estates for the needy, without consideration to the long-term solutions required. As a consequence, whole townships have become run down more quickly than it took them to be built. Even worse, corruption has distorted the help initiatives, with raw materials going missing, and 'smart' occupants renting illegally to untold numbers of people at inflated prices.

Proper analysis of the corrective measures is more important than politically motivated 'showy' solutions. It is important too, that it is recognised that in dealing with homelessness wrongly, discrimination is a likely outcome.

Discrimination is shifted towards a community majority who generally have to struggle for a lifetime to secure home ownership. If we can supply accommodation on Christmas Island for illegal immigrants, we should be able to deliver homes also for the legally homeless in Australia.

To avoid injustice, measures have to be implemented responsibly with regard to homelessness. There is a need for god observation and fact collecting of the problem, done with a sufficiently broad perspective.

Housing assistance invariably draws negative comments. As long as money and profit rule the world, we will need to make big efforts to challenge such a one-sided view. A view that encompasses the betterment of human-life quality should be seen as important also.

Profit through capital builds momentum for 'winners', who remain in a minority compared with the much larger side of 'losers'. Homelessness can be traced back to the 'loser' camp in society. Decisions to change the imbalance will require a majority momentum.

Chapter 23

DIGGING FOR GOLD 3 FEET DEEP

Digging for gold is one thing – digging down 3 feet and actually finding gold, is in the realms of pure luck. Whether it is about the precious end-product of gold, or another gem of value, efforts rarely deliver something of value, quickly.

Travelling into the seemingly empty Australian outback is one place to search for something precious; something which has been long untouched by our modern world. You need to take goods with you which will help you to survive, and tools for digging, like a pick axe and a shovel.

It is compelling for many people to make use of modern equipment. Depending on the finances available this might be a Geiger counter. This is supposed to simplify digging for gold. Reality however proves this wrong, because in order to find gold, there is no doubt; luck is your best companion.

A good example of perseverance in digging for gold is a Kiwi, named Ray. Many years ago, he and his wife May, originally came from Vanuatu to Australia to achieve a better life. With luck, they would achieve this more quickly by finding gold than with regular daily work.

While in Gympie Queensland, the call to try their luck inland found them. Full of enthusiasm, and well-equipped, they joined a surprisingly large number of like-minded 'luck' seekers on a gold site. Making friends was easy, however when stories about finding gold only 3 feet down emerged, the reality of no gain without pain took on new meaning. Ray learned gain came quickly; pain was only waiting around the corner.

In the outback gold field, pain was present even without gain. In winter it was the drought and the extremely cold nights, in summer it was the heat and the unpredictable weather that tested everybody's determination to find gold.

Many diggers lived in either caravans or tents, owned or rented. The tough ones, who had been camped for some time, had made digging for gold a way of life. They had certainly gone past the depth of 3 feet in their search for gold. Complete galleries dug into hillsides or underground told of past and present digging efforts. Lively, colourful stories circulated about how much gold had been found.

Valuable gold always remained hard to come by. Those who found it did so more by accident than anything else. They were the ones who returned to the city to change the gold into money.

What remains from the golden fields, are people who pass on their golden stories. Ray and May, after years on the gold fields, took their stories into a Caboolture caravan park. Their stories of gold digging and finding gold just 3 feet down will probably outlive them, along with stories passed on by others in their story telling.

These stories beg to be written down and preserved for those who come after them, so that future gold-diggers can experience that same excitement too.

Chapter 24

IF LOOKS COULD KILL

What happens if looks could kill? Don't looks spring from our eyes, giving us images of our lives? It is questionable that looks could create such strange outcomes. To explore this, we need to find out how humans might create looks that could kill. To do this we need to listen in on a neighbourhood chat. To this end Mrs Smith meets Mrs Miller at the entrance of their ten storey apartment block.

"Did you hear the noise from across the road? This is outrageous, breaking the peace and quiet of the early morning. This racket really gets on my fragile nerves! We all work through the week, and we need to rest up on the weekend. These people have nothing better to do than to wreck our weekend."

"You are completely right. What can we do about the situation? These people seem to consider that they are more important than us, and they wouldn't listen to us. If the noise continues, we will have no other choice but to lodge an official complaint with the Council."

This exchange of words had hardly come to an end, when the man and his wife from across the road suddenly appeared on the footpath in front of their property. Their clear 'good morning' was lost on the two women, as was the friendly wave they gave, before carrying on down the street.

The women resumed their conversation. "I can't believe that! First the noise, and now this performance!" Both women feel slighted, and their looks send sparks of hard feelings across to the man and his wife. They reflect a lack of understanding, hatred, envy and resentment. These looks are the looks that really could kill.

What is to be learned from this exchange is that whether the looks are designed to hurt or to be kind, most daily situations are usually preceded by a previous history. Keeping this in mind can only help foster better mutual understanding. Lack of communication is often the cause for questionable behaviour.

The philosophical term of 'dichotomy' (bisection) applies to astronomy, particle physics and exists finally in our very own consciousness. A split consciousness can easily lead to socially aberrant behaviour towards our fellow human beings. What triggers the cause is very diverse. In the case of our two female neighbours, a selfish orientation to their world has produced their antisocial behaviours, and affected their perception of the behaviour of others.

Chapter 25

SOMETIMES WHEN YOU DREAM

(poem 100 words only)

Sometimes wishes can come true,
Like a dream is riding a cloud,
High above reality's unforgiving ground.
And when looking down from a distance,
Everything is turning smaller,
Distancing good from bad,
Making us travel further with dreams
Than reality would allow us to go.
Dreams then capture our imagination
With hope, anxiety, joy, but also fear.
Life's moments become extended
In our most secret dreams,
Eventually allowing a window
Into the eternal-dream after life.
But when dreams again dissipate,
Life again has us in a firm grip,
Asking our dreams to come true
In a reality driven world.

(Martin Kari, 2011, Caboolture – Qld. Australien)

Chapter 26

ALMOST A DISASTER

*W*here does a disaster start and end? The answer is of course, where luck cannot reach us anymore, there is a disaster waiting.

In 1977, travelling in Colombia, South America with my wife, and four young children, aged from 3 to 8 years, and our pet dog, an event highlighted how close luck and disaster can sometimes be.

In October, the wet season commences in the tropics of the Southern Hemisphere, where Colombia is located. After a lengthy border crossing at Tulcan, we had finally managed to keep the authorities happy, through a number of toing and froing from Ecuador into Colombia. From this point, it did not take more than half an hour drive on the steep, dusty mountain road to get a first welcoming surprise in Colombia.

We had been told to simply take a border official in our car during our entire passage through Colombia. 'What a privilege!' I thought. I was determined to do something about that. Fortunately, the unexpected encounter in the back of the car with Mars, our German shepherd, gave the official the fright of his life. He immediately agreed to get out of the car after only a short drive. Our dog's panting so close to him, had made him rather frightened. As well, my U.S. dollar note helped him to decide to leave us alone. I could not imagine having to look after this uniformed Colombian official all the way to the Venezuelan border.

Again luck was on our side. As the passage through Colombia got on its way, the slightest delay could have created a disaster for us. We had time lines to keep to. The trip had already advanced into the late afternoon, and daylight was becoming short in supply. The road we were driving on was cut into the mountain side, which fell away steeply below us. On the lee side of the rock wall two men waited, watching us suspiciously as we came closer. Once our Chevrolet station wagon was opposite them, they suddenly raised their arms, throwing something towards us.

Despite the trailer behind us, our powerful car responded quickly to the accelerator. At first, we realized that boards with nails in had just missed the car, passing through the gap between car and trailer. Possibly these criminals had been notified by the border-officials we had rid ourselves of a little earlier. To gain distance, I drove as fast as the road conditions would allow. We must have turned up too early for these road besiegers to place their nail boards onto the road. Driving over the nail boards in already reduced daylight would have forcibly stopped us, allowing a robbery to take palace. Instead luck had been on our side and disaster had been kept at bay.

Further on our way to Bogota, the Colombian capital, we climbed a second lot of mountain ranges in the Andes. We were heading towards the hamlet of Armenia with the car. Most of the time there was no traffic, no wonder, considering the road conditions. If you have a problem here, you are on your own, because you are at a height where most people never go during their entire lives.

The tree line near the Equator is close to 5000 metres. Even if fit people have no problem with the thinner air at this altitude, the carburettor of a car will definitely go on strike because of the lack of oxygen. It is necessary to take the air filter off, fiddle with the carburettor, to keep yourself motoring.

In Armenia, however, the population of the whole place seemed to be on the road. Men wearing 'sombreros' would carry something either on their heads, backs or pull a donkey. A car on the road was at that time a phenomenon. Men with scythes over their shoulders, and bush knives in their hands, casually walked in the middle of the only road the place could offer. I was well-advised to keep the car to their pace. Many eyes scrutinized our car to see what was inside. My wife and children, as well as the German shepherd Mars kept curiosity from the outside to a useful distance. Our luggage, hidden under blankets, was not visible.

The curious eyes looked slightly glassy, most likely from the use of the dark green coca leaves. These were commonly chewed in order to compensate for the pain caused by the lack of oxygen in heights surpassing 5000 metres.

We determined to get through Colombia quickly. A transit permit of 5 days for the car, and 30 days for us, could never have worked out. It seemed as if somebody was after our car. We outsmarted this corruption, and made the passage, believe it or not, in three days. This was in part to the effect of 'Inca-Cola' which unbeknown to us, contained real cocaine. We had been wondering why no tiredness had overcome us. The Colombians "Coca cola" label told us, once we had time to study it, that real cocaine was one of the ingredients The beverage "Coca cola" has its origin in this area of Latin America. Today, the drink is mainly an American enterprise, though maintaining its recipe a secret; it most certainly does not include cocaine.

More bad roads, steep mountain passes, and narrow valleys in lonely tropical jungles, with very few human settlements lay ahead of our next destination, Venezuela. On our way, we couldn't miss the clear signs of braking on the road, directed towards the rocky slope. Far down were the remnants of a yellow bus, looking like a pin head. It must have also become the last resting place for its passengers. All that was left for us was to not lose control of the situation, whereby disaster would be waiting to happen.

widened, and progressed through tunnels, saving us another mountain crossing. This city matched the modern image of other South

A short distance before the capital of Bogota, the road American cities. Heavy rain however spoiled the welcome on that day. Hardly any person could be seen. When we finally saw someone walking on the footpath, we asked for directions.

The young man at first hesitated to come closer to our car. From a distance, he indicated the direction to go, adding "you are in the 'black part' of the city; if you cherish your life, better get out of here as fast as you can". Again we had been lucky, because the heavy rain had kept everybody off the streets.

Before nightfall, we visited a local restaurant on the outskirts of the city. Again curious local eyes looked into our car. Our German shepherd was guarding our belongings, and if people came too close, the dog moved them away. One could never be sure of people's intentions.

The restaurant was packed with locals. Most of them had come on the back of a horse, and had tied them up to special posts in a parking area in front of the restaurant. All men wore sombreros, even inside the restaurant. When I realized this, I went back to the car, to get a sombrero for our heads, too.

In the middle of the smoke filled restaurant a table waited for us. From behind the bar, a bearded man looked with cautious interest towards us. I gave him a friendly wave, which he answered by coming towards us. He said nothing, merely looking around the table at each of us. I broke the silence and asked him if we could have something to eat. Still no word from him. He indicated instead, with his stretched forefinger, the question of how would we be paying. Knowing that people here were after foreign currencies, especially the U.S. dollar, I asked if we could pay with U.S. dollars. 'Dollar' was all he wanted to hear, because the restaurant didn't have any foreign customers. His response surprised me. He passed a flat hand across his throat, indicating what might happen if we had U.S. dollars in our possession.

I responded using the same method: pointing my index finger straight towards him. I hadn't brought my firearm into the restaurant, but I had seen that almost everybody in this exclusive male gathering had a belt around their hip with a holster hanging down their side. The message was understood.

Our dinner was served on a plate, with only one big steak. When attempting to ask what else went with the steak, nobody seemed to understand. Only the sugar cane Schnapps which everyone had in glasses in front of them, was offered. I pointed in a friendly way towards our children, as a way of avoiding this fiery drink. The meat was too much for our stomachs to take, so our farewell from this place did not take long.

Despite pouring rain, people had gathered around our car, trying to catch a glimpse of our dog and belongings. Mars did a good job securing the whole car, especially when he saw us reappear from the restaurant. He ran inside the car to all the windows chasing everybody away.

Daylight had meanwhile given way to night's darkness, obscuring the outside with a heavily clouded sky. A night's sleep in our spacious car was only a consideration for the children. I kept myself behind the steering wheel, while my wife occupied us both with music, conversation, and snacks, as well as the so helpful sip of the local 'Inca-cola' bottle.

Bucaramanga was not far from the boarder of Venezuela any more. Sunny periods gave us a welcomed break from the heavy tropical rain. Here traffic was almost non-existent. Hamlets with small farming communities lived their self-sufficient lives independently from the rest of the world. People, nevertheless, suspiciously kept distance from foreign intruders like us. Children on the side of the stony, dusty road probably could not understand us driving a car, which was not a possibility for them even in their dreams.

Therefore a stone thrown towards the bypassing car must have helped to give vent to their frustrations. On the other hand, having a stone coming through the windscreen in an unsuitable place wasn't really an option for us. A good effective deterrent had to be in place well before a stone was sent on its way. The head of our German shepherd through a side window actually did the trick. You could see how the stone in the hand was dropped to a child's side immediately, probably more out of surprise than of fear. If this hadn't worked, the only other option was to point the gun. Fortunately that was not required.

A shattered windscreen would have amounted to a disaster. There would have been no opportunity for replacement, and in some low lying areas of the rainforest swarms of mosquitos and all imaginable sizes of bugs in the air, we would have been eaten alive in the car.

When we thought we had almost completed this part of our South American tour, another uninvited special incident waited for us. Heavy rain over the past days had created many torrents on the mountain slopes. The road cut its way along rock walls of a deep valley. To the left of us was an abyss of more than 2000 metres, and to the right steep mountain terrain reaching the sky.

Watercourses, small and large were seeking passage everywhere. For most of the day no other car was on the road. Around a bend however, three cars had stopped suddenly on the road, making passage for another car, hazardous if not dangerous. A number of people were also on the road. They pointed with their raised arms towards the rock wall on the side. Mud and water crossed the road in front of us. There was not enough room to drive through. A truck arrived from nowhere at the scene as well. It didn't stop, but rather found a way between the rock wall and the cars, by pushing with its big tyres. For a moment, rushing mud and water was moved off the road. When I saw this, I did not even think about the possible consequences of my actions, there was no time. Instinctively I followed directly behind the truck, in its tyre tracks, before the road closed again with rushing mud.

My car struggled at first to find a grip on the road, but varying the revs helped immediately to get us through for a certain distance. My biggest worry was the trailer behind our car, as it might lose traction and pull the car towards the abyss.

Just as we had successfully left the muddy stretch of the road, disaster struck behind us. In my rear vision mirror, I saw the whole mountain rock wall crashing across the road into the valley abyss, sending the other three cars and the people on a journey to their graves. Help here was so distant, that nothing was possible to assist. Those people had simply disappeared into the Colombian jungle.

I continued driving slowly, another kilometre or so, until a cove into the mountain side gave me room to stop. My knees were shaking when I left the car. Was it the positive thinking of our children in the back of the car that had guided us unharmed through this deadly trap? Our eldest son, Risto, aged eight years, reassured us confidently "I wasn't afraid, because I knew we'd make it." Such a positive attitude may have helped to keep disaster once more at bay. Appreciation of life went up a few notches at this point. An outcome only this sort of experience could deliver.

The Colombian/Venezuelan border came closer. As soon as we came down from the mountains, onto the plains around Lake Maracaibo in the middle of the night, wet and steamy heat hit us like a hammer. The mountains surrounding Lake Maracaibo kept the heat and humidity constant. It was 45C with humidity that almost glued eyelids to eyeballs, with persistent insect swarms which welcomed new arrivals in the mouth, ears and everywhere else possible.

What a change I thought. A few hours earlier we had been up in the mountains not far from the snow line and now we were in hell's oven. Cucuta was the border town. Near the official border crossing, the night was lit up with a spotlight. When we stopped on the side of the widened road under a flowering jacaranda, almost instantly officials in green uniforms came towards us leaving their hut with door and windows open.

Their Spanish words broke the silence, while swarms of insects carried their messages to us into the car. "Interesting travel set up, we need to check everything you have; where are your passports, leave them with us." I told them in Spanish that I would bring our passports to their office. We could not afford to lose our passports.

Inside the hut/office one officer sat respectfully at a desk, requesting that I leave the passports with him, and that I remain outside his office. I watched with satisfaction that our 'jeito' hadn't failed, and that he had found the U.S. dollar note in the back of my passport.

Here we saw that all these officials were chewing fresh green coca leaves to help them withstand the terrible heat. Their eyes were matte and watery. After a lot of storytelling, we were able to leave this border post. No-one else could be seen.

Back at our car, we allowed ourselves some quick refreshment and a cup of coffee which my wife had prepared at our trailer. We could not rest even for a few moments to regain some strength from our near disasters. The climate made you feel like your blood was boiling; head and heart did not know what was going on. Never had we experienced worse climatic conditions.

After the official farewell of the Colombian border officials with a hand-salute off their military caps, we quickly found that air coming in through the car windows, as we drove, helped our well-being. This was only possible though when the insects came in and managed to get out straight away on the opposite window side.

We knew that the road leading up into the mountains would bring more relief with moderate climatic conditions. Therefore, we pushed on. After about half an hour I wondered what had happened to the border crossing into Venezuela. Was it possible we had missed it? We needed to stop, and go back a certain distance to find out.

And what did we find? We indeed had passed an even smaller hut on the side of the road. Two officials were asleep inside and the boom-gate had been left up so that no disruption would occur for the officers' siesta. When we dared to wake the two officers, they were rather upset demanding that everything be taken out of our car and trailer. The 'jeito' (reached agreement) and their readiness to doze away again, kept our border stop within reasonable time. I managed even to present myself as a VIP-person who had arrived from Germany to visit this great country of Venezuela. They liked this and let us proceed.

It was in La-Guaira, on the coast near the capitol of Caracas, when again leaving Venezuela, we learned that without the entry stamps into the country we could not have left Venezuela.

Back to our entry into the country from Colombia, we were then free to carry on to higher areas. The mountain Pico Bolivar rises here to a height of just over 5000 metres. It did not take us long to again find cooler air. A final lucky encounter with 'campesinios', the rural population, brought this part of our adventure, which had hovered close to disasters, to a temporary end. A stretch of bitumen road lead into dense forest, away from the main road. This invited us to stop during the night and have a sleep for a change.

The place we had chosen was well-hidden and difficult for anyone to see us. This was what we thought, until well into the hours of morning when someone looked through our car windows with a smile on their face.

We indeed had slept right through the night, and well into the next day. Only a little sunlight made it through the dense jungle. We received not only a warm welcome, but also an invitation into a nearby rainforest hut of a family that lived there. No questions were asked, and we were offered a shower in their special bathroom, and invited to share some food at their table.

The shower was an interesting set up. Hanging bamboo mats made up a small, square room, while from the ceiling hung a leather bag filled with rainwater. Untying a knot at the bottom of the bag released the water. Everything was simple, orderly and functional.

After the shower, we sat down with the couple in their hut. Everything was made from what the jungle could supply. The hut didn't need closed windows at this altitude of the jungle. During the day the sun warmed the air comfortably before becoming sufficiently cool for sleeping at night. We were simply touched by this unselfish welcome from people with little possessions.

An outside display of cattle skins on horizontal bamboo cane strung between trees was the main business of the couple. It was here, that skins rubbed in salt, were dried in the jungle. They were protected from the heat of the sun, and kept under cool, moist conditions which in turn meant the best leather was produced. The farmers' cattle were running freely over a large area of rain forest.

It came time to say farewell, as the day had already advanced close to midday. The farmer joined us on the short walk to our car. He explained to us that they had rich soil to grow everything that they needed, and also the ground provided bitumen freely. The pressure from the nearby oil fields around Lake Maracaibo sent the oil up through the soil, to the extent that they only had to run a steam roller over the surface and a bitumen road was ready.

CONCLUSION

There are many ways to look at a disaster. Events from the real world show us that a disaster can always be just around the corner. We can collect experiences and learn useful answers that can help in the event of a close encounter with disaster. If we sit on the side lines of life, in most cases we are left unprepared for the unexpected. How people react can worsen or relieve a disaster. Natural disasters of course are a different issue altogether. There is nothing we can do about them, other than to hope that this kind of disaster doesn't happen to us.

NATURE'S CATHEDRAL

(Poem: Martin Kari)

The city - concrete jungle - lies a long way back,
single houses are left behind, too.
A road - beaten tracks - fields, meadows – all have disappeared.
In a green wall nature's stronghold rises out of its jungle.
Somewhere bush stoops low, allowing passage on foot into obscurity.
Leaves, branches, lianas barricade the interior,
little tree trunks lock-up space, whereas here and
there large tree trunks rise up straight, holding a
dark roof canopy high into the sky,
leaving little room for sunlight to shine through.
The catbird invisibly mews his penetrating warning,
an intruder has arrived in nature's rainforest cathedral.

A voice, a breaking branch under a foot, all noises
are carried a long way, high up through the canopy,
everything has stopped and is watching from a hiding place.
On the ground, wallabies, possums, tree-kangaroos,
bandicoots, cuscus, brush-turkeys, goannas,
pythons, tree-snakes, lizards and geckos.
And in mid-area in young treetops : beetles,

butterflies, spiders, and insects.
Cicadas' chirping moves in waves across the forest
cathedral, announcing the rain soon to come.
Some of nature's most colourful creatures, king
parrots, rainbow lorikeets, kingfishers, sunbirds,
riflebirds, honeyeaters, regent bowerbirds,
all watch the intruder from high up in the canopy.
All are present in the cathedral, but nothing the
eye initially can meet.

Only when silence has returned,
all creatures large and small start life's daily routines
again, moving, searching, feeding on what the rainforest holds,
sometimes playing, resting, waiting.
Silence of the permanent residents is then broken,
telling each other the different stories with sharp
calls, long songs and noises.
A visitor can observe more near the ground after
the eye has adjusted to dim daylight.
Moist cooler air stores in a constant exchange the
rain in the ground, feeding hopeful young plant life
with fallen leaves, branches and trees.
Bird-nest ferns and stag-horns form leaf-cups high
up in trees to catch light and moisture.

A wait-a-while creeper makes the hasty visitor wait
for a while to lick his wounds from nasty itchy sting.
Then a massive tree-trunk in the way stops the
visitor, sending his eyes upwards to look how far he can see.
Some trees spread with flat triangular roots on the
forest-floor, increasing the support of a jungle-giant on the ground.
Huge strangler figs often dominate other tree-giants

with their massive trunk roots growing from the
top of a host-tree all the way around downwards.
When reaching the ground, the host-tree's fate is sealed,
the fig strangles the host.
Some trunk-roots of a strangler become so huge
that passages between allow you to walk through.
Old solid lianas also come down from old trees,
Often in loops to block a passage.
They never say 'swing on me'.
When crushing down from a dwindling height,
only then will we know, how firm, large and heavy
they were, endangering somebody underneath for sure.
Fungi, mosses, ants, snails often hide under leaves on the ground.
All life here is told not to make a mistake.
And so the visitor is also bound to do, when he
wants to see something and stay safe from the
rainforest's natural defences wait-a-while, snakes,
spiders, accidentally fallen branches.

Very few flowers develop in this darkness,
umbrella trees with their long umbrella-formed
leaves specially attract lorikeets to their distinct
red flower-studs, creating with the honey-licking
lorikeets an incredible colour paradise.
A goanna can rarely be seen, often in a sunny spot,
soaking up the warmth.
When disturbed, they rush in haste
up a tree-trunk.
Watching them already reveals that they sense
their direct environment with their constant
searching, thin long tongue, an encounter with ancient prehistory.

*In nature's cathedral many trees establish an
existence over a long period of time and can
therefore often be found today only in one place.
Rainforests in Australia are the oldest on earth,
harbouring the richest variety in living forms
despite the small remaining forest pockets.
Black apple, red cedar, bunya pine, trees still
growing after hundreds of years into rainforest
giants, tree ferns usually come up in penetrating
light-corridors, giving the lower forest area a fine
green shine against the mostly dark-brown an
dark-green forest shades.
Lower areas of a rainforest can harbour a
watercourse. Palms near a water-flow add a tropical image to the forest.*

*Water usually leaves a forest,
starting a journey through countryside, mostly
without the protection of the forest.
Only a constant supply from the forest gives a river
the start for its journey.
Without it, a river ceases to exist.
Time in a rainforest cathedral seems to stop.
Birds from the high canopy tell with their voices
when morning and nightfall arrive.
In the night's darkness many rainforest residents
waken to life, possums, geckos, bandicoots, bats,
seeking the cooler hours.
To leave the rainforest cathedral during the day is
to bring back the open heat of the land.*

*The rainforest is a cathedral, a quiet place, where
high trees support its roof, creating a huge dome*

under which life finds protection.
Visiting a rainforest cathedral gives us back nature's
very basic strength for our body and mind.
We have an obligation to preserve what is left of the rainforest.
So that future generations can also experience this paradise on earth.
When leaving the rainforest cathedral, the green wall
of nature's jungle remains behind unchanged.
Meadows, fields, beaten tracks, roads bring us closer
to single houses again and finally back to our own
jungle creation, the city concrete jungle.

(Martin Kari-2009-Caboolture-Australia)

FROM THE FAWQ POETRY EDITOR'S DESK

This poem by Martin Kari is a prose poem, which is a combination of prose and poetry. It is not 'free verse' which is a more contracted form. Prose poetry generally is written very much from the heart. It does not concern itself too much with form and line ending. It aims at telling the truth. It has variable lengths and is often written in story style. It does not try to be very clever, constantly inviting stress to find fresh metaphor, smile. It generally tells what it wants to in plain language. The poet expresses a strong desire to share with the reader what he sees, how he feels. The prose poem is comfortable in its telling, not having to rely on the hammered 'show don't tell'. We get a clear message.

Readers of this poem will experience with the poet his joy in his observations of what nature is showing/providing for him. We cannot help but enter the rainforest with him and be rewarded.

Baudelaire (French poet, 1821-1867, Paris) was renowned for his prose poems. Martin very much follows in modern terms with this poem.

(Caroline Glen – May 2009)

Chapter 28

A GLORIOUS DAY

(Poem: Martin Kari)

*Silence still rules over the night.
The moon has travelled its path.
It sits at the horizon, waiting to change
nightlight into sunny daylight.
The net of little starlight holes in the sky have shone
distant messages to resting dark Mother Earth.*

*A new day is every time born when
the fiery sun looks over the bowed far horizon.
First, in a dark blue shimmering haze,
adopted by growing red ribbon-flame walls,
then lightening bush, trees and houses send their
long, dark shades on to wider spreading ground.*

*Vanishing shade-creations accompany silence,
stepping back with time to allow bright orange
sunlight to finally flood all the chosen land
with daylight in a piercing yellow disc;
this time through a sky, free of barricading
clouds, now an azure-blue spectacle.*

First, in the air, a cautious birdsong,
then on the ground, life begins a daily routine,
following the rule: the early bird catches
the worm. People, too hear this call, everything seems
to move with them into the awakening morning hours.

Cosy, sunny warmth out of the sky reconciles with
a chilly night, eating away foggy mist to prepare a
glorious day. More bright sunlight rises into the sky,
all creatures rush, rest, move restless vehicles,
more people are moved in buses, trains and further
away even our own 'bird-mimics' take into the air.

Silence of the night has then gone into hiding
where it is safe from this daily human hubbub. Nature
still holds the key to recharge our 'batteries' in its
oases of forests, wilderness, where land meets a
river or the ocean, mountains, sometimes even green
blossoming city-parks and homey surroundings.

Nature still offers to escape from our hubbub into its
oases. Then a far cry from daily pressures, life can worship
a glorious day. Everything and everybody
recognises this from an office, a workshop, in an open
field, the athlete, the sick, the rich, the poor,
the young and the old.

Difficulties then hide in our memories, giving wings
to a new, better hope. Because the sun has taken the reigns of the
day, generously shines indiscriminately, quietly onto our lucky spot,
Mother Earth. All we see, know, is accidental. The 'glory' around
us highlighted by the sun, reconciles us also with little sunshine.

*Life has never been all sunshine. We grab the sunny
moments of life or go down the road of despair.
Day's warmth finally slips into the first hours
after midday, keeping it up for all afternoon.
Then the sun hovers towards the horizon again,
resending its longer shadow-creations.*

*And so do all daily rush-hours, following into a
calmer evening and prepare night-silence to return.
The balmy night not hints at the chill yet to come,
while the sun's farewell carry cooler hours with
a bite in the air, sending many of us back into houses, where
our artificial lights attempt to replace the sun.*

*Life still carries on, but slowly is taken over by silence,
and daylight creatures worship a rest time,
upon which the enlightened stars, the moon-face keep
equal vigilance over remaining activities; over
a sleeping world, too, which prepares for another
glorious day. Moon shine and let also rest the sun.*

Chapter 29

GOLDEN 'ABITUR'

'All roads lead to Rome' and in that sense March 24 in 2012 many roads also lead to the town of Ettlingen in the South of Germany. Fifty years have gone by since the classes A/B/C of the Eichendorff-Gymnasium have gone on many journeys during their lives after the 'Abitur' in 1962.

The call to come home was heard by a number of the former school students. By chance this call reached even the Antipodes. Sunshine greeted this gathering on the footpath in front of the Gymnasium on that Saturday.

Well ahead of the agreed time to meet, the first serious contenders arrived. After handshakes were exchanged, introductions follow likewise: "I am Axel Hildiger, class A, you are probably from one or the other class; also from class A, am I right?"

The gathering continues. First memories are exchanged from a time, now decades back. Meanwhile at the glass front door the school headmistress arrives from the inner courtyard of the surrounding u-shaped buildings. Though slowly moving the gathered group arrives at the entrance also. At a quick estimate about 40 former students from classes A/B/C have arrived.

A colourful bouquet of flowers is presented to Mrs Messmer, the former headmistress. In return, she proudly announces that there are

900 hopeful students also visiting the school. The eastern wing of the school still contains the former classrooms of fifty years ago. At the invitation of the headmistress, we follow her to this area. Along corridors with views through walls of glass we move to the inner courtyard. The congregation gains access to one of the former classrooms. Today this room accommodates a very modern 'physics' teaching area.

Mrs Messmer asks if anyone has any questions, considering it's fifty years since we were here. In her opening remarks, Mrs Messmer states that teachers today do not use the cane on pupils' hands anymore. This brings to mind memories of past experiences. One of the past students recounts a story.

"We were no angels, occasionally I would cause the light into the classroom to disappear, by fusing one of the power points with an electrical wire. No light in the classroom meant the lesson had to be interrupted until the power outage could be restored. This did not mean the culprit was found however." On a more positive note, the headmistress didn't fail to mention that the new generation of attendees still received the 'Nuremberg Funnel' (the funnel to feed the brain) as in the past.

Back in the school yard, cameras catch pictures of who is left of the Golden-Abitur classes. All are encouraged to 'smile please'. This is the close of the official side of the 'Golden Abitur' celebration, and everyone is ushered to the exit doors, with best wishes for the future.

The next activity on the program starts at the Sun Hotel in Pforzheimer Street. During a leisurely walk through the town's centre, the assembled group divide into small groups. The pleasant sunshine of this year's early spring invites many to relax at tables and seats set up on the footpaths, which in some places extend out into the middle of the road. For a short time the Golden Abitur participants merge with other sun seekers in the town's centre, only to meet up later at the Sun Hotel. Their number has now grown to nearly sixty.

Despite the crowded situation at the restaurant, the owner manages to satisfy the gourmet wishes of everyone. Once more past and present stories are shared, along with plates of delicious food, and glasses of drink.

Having satisfied the needs of hunger, the meeting moves outside the Hotel, where Axel Hildinger, a medical doctor from nearby Malsch shares his historical knowledge of the old part of Ettlingen. He surprised everyone with his well-founded knowledge of former personalities such as Thibault, as well as his knowledge of the history of the town gates, the town walls, the Jesuit College which once accommodated our first grammar school, and has now been taken over by the Finance Department. Previously the finance section had used the former classrooms of A/B/C when they moved into the newly built Eichendorff Gymnasium in December, 1957.

Memories return of events during school lessons of the past. One memory is stirred of a particular Biology lesson, which was conducted on the surrounding forest hill, called Robberg. During this excursion, a Council street cleaner, nicknamed 'Stadtlaucher', heard the name of Martin as a class member. There was an incident with some students which infuriated the council worker, who then identified Martin, as the chief culprit to the class teacher. Our teacher, Mr Borger immediately paid attention to the worker. This was followed by a good hiding being dispensed to Martin in front of the whole class. The class was then told to return to school and as a general punishment to the whole class, there was to be a written lesson in maths. This was how the teacher vented his anger.

What occurred on that day, continued on to the next. Slowly it leaked out that Martin wasn't the culprit at all. As a result of this new information, Mr. Borger took the opportunity to congratulate Martin on his best math's results, but also stated that Martin had earned a credit for a thrashing in the future. This is how relations between school staff and students could be managed, fifty years ago.

The net activity as part of the anniversary was devoted to dinner together in a restaurant called Kulinarium, situated opposite the former

Rhineland Barracks. Until the dinner, everyone had free time and could enjoy the unusually beautiful weather however they liked. One group decided to pay the museum within the castle of former Countess Sibilla a visit.

Here there were any remarkable exhibits, but several aged pianos drew special attention. Under the skilled hands of a museum clerk, the group was shown how previous 'technology' helped the playing of classical music by means of a 'punched' paper tape.

Memories continue to be shared, and prior to the joint dinner, the reality of life becomes evident when we realize the number of fellow classmates who have not made it this far in life, because of illness or accidents. Moments of silence help to remember them also.

A fellow classmate, Dieter Steinmetz contributes some memories of school times. Martin, now from Australia also adds his anecdotes to the sharing of stories from class A. Martin is able to participate in the celebrations, due to the hospitality of Dirk Waninger.

Martin remembers:

Early veggies from North Morocco.......first warning..... what is your achievement in maths....no way....this is not clear enough.... The task must be tickled out... (Watzke)

Such gang of a sow I've never seen in all my life, sit down, get up, remain standing straight! Jesus, you are and remain immature pupils... ('Appendix', Helmut Weh)

Boy, go cutting wood... look at the size of my hand... you better not come close to it! (Dr. Gerlich)

Ah, you certainly could have done better than that...Ah, I mean it... ('Babette'Frl. Zollner)

> *Schulz, I'm not your babysitter... I've seen, what my eyes have picked up... I rather have a close examination of my own at home... a good Sunday catch... (Frl. Wetz)*
>
> *Men, get lost ... from nothing comes nothing... (Herr Fuß)*
>
> *Hallelujah Amalia figure of Christ! Go visiting the pub in Malsch, get yourself a beer and a sausage... show off on Sunday in your best confirmation suit... but don't come into my sport lesson, you yokel... You expect from your teacher Kirsch, a father of five innocent children, to be with one foot in prison... chief teacher Danner, future people educator... Riedlinger, Latin excellent, sports no good at all... (Otto Kirsch)*

The Martin, who put all this together, after 65 years of age, became an internationally recognized author; writing books not only in the German language, but also in English. Teachers once gave Martin rather unsatisfactory reports, yet that was school, this is now what he had achieved. Questions are inevitable at this point.

In the past 5 years initially 12 English books were published worldwide with renowned publishers. Then in the following 5 years the same books were rewritten and published in the German language.

How time can change predictions of the past.

All things though come to an end, and thus the celebration of the Golden Abitur finishes. The farewell from this gathering takes place more or less in slow motion, contrary to the welcoming at the beginning.

Everybody shares the well wishes for a continued happy journey in life. Another 65 year celebration is even mentioned! Time only will tell who will then be a part of that.

Chapter 30

A "BLIND CHOOK" FINDS ITS CORN

The teacher of Latin and German, at the honoured Ettlingen Gymnasium admonished Martin and Dirk: "If the penny doesn't drop with you today, there is still hope, and that like 'the blind chook' you will eventually find the corn!"

Until 2010, Dirk and Martin had spent years together, sitting on the same school benches, and sharing a great friendship. In the many years since school, Dirk's life had taken place mostly within Europe, while Martin had lived his post-school years on four continents. These included Europe, Africa, South America and finally settling with his family, in Australia.

A second opportunity to share friendship occurred for the two friends. Dirk, with his wife Ottilie, paid a visit to Martin in Australia. As when items are 'double stitched' it is said to make things stronger. This also can apply to a friendship.

Dirk's first visit to Australia goes back to 1981. It was in the summer month of December, when in a hobby capacity Dirk guided a group of overseas visitors to Queensland. This group were potential investors into sugarcane farming. Dirk's knowledge of English was particularly helpful in establishing communication with the locals.

On this occasion, Dirk knocked also on the door of Martin's newly established home. Martin had only recently migrated from Germany to Australia. For Dirk it was an opportunity to see at close hand, the better life Martin believed he had achieved. During his visit and even though the guest resisted, Dirk was honoured at a dinner in the Bavarian bratwurst restaurant in Brisbane's city centre.

During this visit, it gave Martin and Dirk a chance to unpack their memory boxes and relive some of the mutual experiences of their shared past. These were experiences such as years with the Boy Scout movement and an early expedition around the Mediterranean, including the Middle East and North Africa.

It was in 1967 that the then young men had been encouraged by the shining example of the local newspaper agent, who then was located in KronenstraBe, to go on that tour, even though they had little funds. The gentleman from the local newspaper rode the whole tour on his bicycle. Reports of his tour appeared regularly in the newspaper. Dirk and Martin however, didn't have that much time available to go by cycle. Instead they created out of two VW-bus wrecks one useful vehicle, which was to take them successfully on the journey. There were many challenges on the tour, given that during this time, tourists were hardly seen in this part of the world.

Without doubt, this kind of adventure helped to prepare the path for finding the 'corn' of life. For both Martin and Dirk, life after school had continued their learning. Both continued on with a successful basic technical education in an apprenticeship; this was then followed by University.

All of this was regardless of the questions raised about their learning by teachers during their school days. Dirk went on to succeed with his own consultancy business, assisting high tech companies, operating from Kassel.

On the other hand Martin entered a new chapter of his life, post retirement at the age of 65. The 'corn' for Martin came in the successful guise of becoming an internationally recognized author.

The lesson from this is as follows: It is never too late in a lifetime, to undertake something new. Martin currently has to his credit, written and published 8 English language texts covering a range of subject. This has been also followed by 8 German language texts. Where there is enjoyment, success is also possible.

Dirk's second visit to Australia occurred in April, 2010. Again they both celebrated their individual achievements, since their last visit. Martin continues to appreciate the quality of life Australia offers. With its natural tropical backdrop, the north-eastern part of Queensland invites all to experience one of the last paradises on Earth. Along the eastern shore, two and a half thousand kilometres of Pacific Ocean coastline follows a parallel inland green carpet of rainforest on the Great Dividing Range up to New Guinea in the north.

The blue-green water of the Pacific, with its white wave crests washes the fine golden sandy beaches, while keeping the largest and richest coral reef in abundant sea life. It is a beauty balanced by danger.

The most ancient tropical rainforests on earth are still in existence in isolated parts of Queensland. Ancient life forms continue to exist, such as: the platypus, echidna, cassowary, wallaby, possum and wombat, along with a multitude of bird life. Birds such as, parrots, rainbow lorikeets, kookaburras, catbirds, frogmouths and many more, continue to thrive.

In what has remained of these ancient rainforests, gigantic trees protect young tree life with contained humidity and reduced daylight. Since primeval times, the largest tree specimens which still stand are the curtain fig tree, strangler fig, hoop pine, bunya pine and red and white cedar to name a few. These continue to find shelter at varying heights under the rainforest canopy. It is this natural environment which teaches us about natural order.

Martin's lyric poem, 'Rainforest Cathedral' aims to give the reader a shared experience of his visit in this species diverse and aged rainforest.

In the past 29 years that Martin has lived on this fifth continent, he and his family have undertaken several tours right across, and around

Australia. His books: 'Road to Nitmiluk' (Australian ruft), and 'One Migrant Experience' (Aus & Ein-Wandern) provide a good insight into Australia.

Dirk also has collected world-wide experiences since school days. Both men enjoy sharing their learnings about their real life adventures of Australia, Martin's insight leaves us with memories of the unspoiled environment of a distant continent. With population mostly concentrated in large cities, changes to nature and its sensitive environment, have been mostly avoided.

While we have looked very generally at the Sunshine State of Queensland, we must also give attention to the particular area where Martin and his family call home. Fifteen kilometres outside the county town of Caboolture lies the family property, a far cry from hectic city life. On one hectare, originally farming land, the family built their dream home with their own hands. With time, a veranda was added to go completely around the house along with the must have workshop, kid's playhouse, parrot cages, storage sheds and last but not least, a room for an indoor swimming pool with shower/toilet facility. The sauna being a must have in at least half of every Finnish household.

Almost all year round, our life can take place outdoors. Whether for work, or recreation, entertaining or socializing, all is possible. Around the house, the tropical garden creates views into paradise. All year round, it is warm enough to live outside the house, while the veranda fulfils the task of keeping the Queensland summer sun in check. The well-built and insulated house serves also as a means to escape from excessive heat, and provides the opportunity to get a good night's sleep.

When visiting Martin in 'Downunder', Dirk and Ottilie were reassured that Martin had indeed found his 'corn' during his life. As a farewell present to Dirk and his wife, Martin's neighbours, Gordon and Tina, took all for a four wheel drive tour along the sandy beaches of the Pacific, just north of their property.

The rolling waves of the Pacific Ocean spill onto mostly wide uninhabited beaches, leaving the sand wet enough, and firm enough for a vehicle to drive on. Off the coast line, within visible distance, north to south, are the sandy islands of Frazer, Bribie, Moreton and Stradbroke. The first three we were able to visit, before Dirk and Otti's departure.

A ferry boat takes visitors from the mainland across to the northerly situated Frazer Island. After a short trip, one can see the open Pacific Ocean side: white foam on wave crests washing the golden sand, with the beach line remaining wide even at high tide. On stretches, you can see the partly raised shore line with the coloured sands of Rainbow Beach towards the island's interior. Dense, green forests cover the island. Looking back over the island, westward, this lively, green carpet continues on to mountain ranges, which run parallel to the coast. Occasionally a pointed mountain sticks out, indicating its volcanic origin. Above all this stretches a blue sky, in which the glowing disc of the sun keeps an eye on this paradise.

Further south, Bribie Island is located, sitting only a little apart from the mainland. Here a bridge crosses from the mainland to the island. Contrary to Frazer Island, the other three islands are mostly populated, however the natural scenery of ocean, beach, forests and mountain ranges are protected for all to admire.

A ferryboat brings visitors to Moreton and Stradbroke. Moreton is unique in its position opposite the metropolitan area of Brisbane. It gives an astonishing view from unspoiled sandy beaches against a backdrop of coco palms, across crystal clear blue-green sea water towards skyscrapers, which announce the city profile.

One particular volcanic mountain Mount Glorious stands out clearly against the cityscape, showing off its uninterrupted green rainforest cover. Where else in the world can we experience a view of the unspoiled subtropics against a neighbouring urban civilization. Such images leave lasting memories, as well as encourage us to continue our lives more confidently.

For Dirk and Ottilie, their return to Germany was imminent. For them, springtime was starting to prepare to welcome them back to Kassel, with its surrounding meadows and deciduous forests. After these travel experiences, both Martin and Dirk, 'these chooks' have overcome their blindness in finding their own corn, post school. To what degree have the comments of the Latin and German teachers motivated them? In the end, everything has turned out well, so there must have been some positives. The memories of home remind them of what they have gained, and where they both really stand in life. Contentedness is the achievement of overcoming controversies and distances.

It is the writer's intention to open the eyes of others and show that even 'blind chooks' can find their 'corn', with the help of a long standing friendship.

Chapter 31

CHRISTMAS ONCE UPON A TIME

"Martin get ready. We are going to select a Christmas tree in our surrounding Black Forest." The year is 1948, and I have permission from the Forestry Department to cut one Christmas tree out of the nearby tree nursery. Enough moon light shines tonight, to light our way through the deep white snow fields. "Make sure you are dressed for the cold, with a wool cap over your ears; close your jacket right up under your chin; trousers over your shoes so that the snow cannot reach your socks nor your feet." We will be on foot through the forest snow fields. "Here is also a piece of chocolate, best kept in your jacket pocket for when you wish to refresh yourself. Are you ready? Let's make sure we stay close together. Don't forget your gloves either," Peter tells his son.

While on foot, the silence invites a story. Dad can look back on quite a number of years of his life where he has experienced special Christmas preparations, particularly when he was young. The reminiscing makes the time on foot pass in a flash.

A bright, full moon shines in the sky. Its light shows spaces between dark green fir-islands. Silence reigns here. No birds or forest animals are about. All creatures sleep in hidden places. Only two people, a father with his son, leave their footsteps in the untouched newly fallen snow.

The depth of the snow still allows walking. Branches of the larger fir trees are laden heavily with snow, forcing the branches to point to the ground. Some, very near the ground, have dropped their snow caps and added to the snow mass in that area. Because of this, a path has to be selected away from the fir trees, more or less between rows of them.

After a while, up and downhill, a forest clearing shows a small growth fir nursery. Only one of the trees has reached the height of an adult. Dad selects a tree which is easy to access, at the start of the nursery. In his rucksack waits a handsaw.

"While I cut this dense tree just above the snow surface, you stay to the side. Watch the tree as it falls to the ground, and make sure it doesn't hit you. At first we will both grab the tree in the middle of its trunk, and shake off most of the snow caps. Are you ready? Let's first shake the trunk, backwards and forwards, together."

'Look how the snowflakes fly into our faces,' shouts Martin excitedly.

"Keep your gloves on; the snow is cold, especially when we move the snow at the bottom of the trunk. Moving it will help me cut the base. Martin, despite what I said earlier to you, I might have you hold this little tree while I start cutting. Do you think you can hold it steady?"

'Of course I can,' Martin reassures his Dad.

"I know you are a strong boy, let's go ahead! When the tree is cut I will help you to put it slowly on to the ground. The rope in my rucksack will help bind the tree, and make it smaller in order to carry it home. Each of us will hold one end of the tree. I will go first with the heavier end, and you will follow holding up the tree top." We proceed and the job is soon done with all going to plan.

"Let us go back the same way as we took coming here. If you need a rest, don't hesitate to let me know. It won't take that much longer to return home. The moon is still shining brightly, and our path is fully lit. We only have to look for our footsteps in the snow."

Not only a bright, slightly yellow moon shows the two Christmas tree-lumberjacks the way home, but also a number of tiny star lights glitter in the dark sky. We soon return to the road down into the valley. The snow here has been pushed to the road side, and home is not far away any more. We now have to pay attention for traffic, but fortunately this has dropped considerably due to the hour.

The closer we get to home, the heavier the tree seems to become. It is with a sigh of relief that Martin releases the Christmas tree in the apartment's living room. A metal stand waits on the floor for the base of the tree trunk, which will become fixed with three evenly spaced screws into the tube for the trunk. The top of the fir tree just fits under the ceiling.

For the remaining days before Christmas Eve, the tree is secretly decorated by Father Christmas's helpers. Silver, as well as golden, stars, colourful little balls, and gingerbread cut into shapes of star, heart or bell are evenly distributed throughout the greenery. They hang on a fine thread from the limbs.

For many years prior to 2015, wax candles were also fitted into shiny holders so that the fir needles would not catch fire. Finally tinsel is draped from branch to branch, stepwise upwards, ending up on the top tip where a golden star fixed with a piece of wire stands out.

After this preparation gifts are placed on the floor, under the tree. Until Christmas Eve, the room where the decorated tree is found, remains locked, so that it will be a surprise for the children who are present.

On Christmas Eve, winter usually likes to send white snowflakes out of an obscure sky. Most activities have stopped for the festive season, and people, both young and old dedicate their energies to a higher task, namely to give joy to others.

A green, fresh tree in a family home brings nature close to daily life, at least for Christmas. After the preparation of the Christmas tree, and the locking of the room, Martin can't wait much longer, and he asks impatiently, more than once a day, "when is Santa Claus coming to me?"

Mother responds gently, 'When you have been a good boy all year round, then Santa will include you in his visit to all the good people.

He leaves presents under the tree, and tonight on Christmas Eve he will go from house to house, ringing his bell when he has finished. This is then the time that everybody in our family is dressed festively to pay respect to Father Christmas. Come with me and I'll give you a final help with your dressing.'

The door from the kitchen allows a first glance into the living room, where the Christmas tree is in full candlelight. The tree shines beautifully in colours of green, silver, gold and much more. Right from the beginning this is an invitation to contribute something to the scene.

"Martin, show us how good you can play your Christmas songs on the flute, and then Mum and Dad will join you with singing the songs. Very nice, now tell us a little Christmas poem which you have learnt at school, and then Mum will add a story."

The candles send out just enough light so that Mum can read her story. Then it's time to look under the Christmas tree, and see what Father Christmas has left behind. Colourfully wrapped packages of different sizes lay around the tree on the floor. Mum encourages Martin to look for the name which appears on one parcel after another.

There is no holding back any more, everybody takes a present, and if it doesn't have the correct name on it, well it is passed on to the right person. More and more wrapping paper piles up under the tree.

Out comes a book, a meccano building set, a special set of new clothes, chocolate as well as marzipan sweets, a hand tool for Dad, colour pencils, a specially painted picture, written words on paper expressing thanks, or wishes or even fantasies. Martin cannot even resist in helping himself to the gingerbread shapes off the tree.

Meanwhile Mum has retreated to the kitchen to prepare Christmas dinner. A good watch has also to be constantly kept on the tree candles so that they do not burn too low in their holders and set fire to the tree.

Next on the program is the Christmas dinner. The table in the lunch room is covered with a silken table cloth. Two candle sticks stand apart in the centre, and mimic the Christmas tree, with a few little fir tree branchlets also on display. Soup and dinner plates are neatly stacked in front of every seat, along with cutlery, glassware, and ornately folded serviettes.

Little Martin still has to learn to eat in a well behaved manner at the festive table. He has to be reminded to keep his arms close to his body, not to lean his elbows on the table and to make sure he doesn't make strange noises while eating and drinking.

Soup, roasted turkey, a variety of vegetables, wine for the adults, and apple juice for Martin, and for dessert a chocolate pudding keep the festivity going. Conversation extends dinner time well into the night.

Martin is already rubbing his eyes from tiredness. Before heading to bed however, he wants again to see all his Christmas presents in the nearby room. A room now filled also with the scent of the fir tree needles.

Time on Christmas Eve has passed quickly for everybody, as if a dream. Thinking of each other, and giving to one another has created joy and satisfaction; something to remember until the next Christmas turns up. Nevertheless the night is late, and because of the earlier excitement, everyone starts to think about going to bed, to ease their tiredness.

When everything is at its best, this is the time for things to finish.

The next morning, it is full daylight as the family rubs the sleep from their eyes. The atmosphere is changed from the candle lit fir tree of the evening before. Martin is first out of bed. He cannot wait to go to his presents, to try things out, build things, read and also use his coloured pens.

Christmas is a special time for family, and helps make up for time lost in the year.

Chapter 32

FACES IN THE STREET

Nothing is still in the street, everything is moving. Is there an escape? Is someone being rescued? Even at night in the artificial daylight, movement, movement, movement.

During the day, cars and their inmates choke the roads. Not so many pedestrians on the major roads, people choose quieter streets, less busy places. People walk past one another, while small groups remain standing in conversation. The people in a hurry appear very important. Most carry baggage, either by hand or over the shoulder, or on their backs; a handbag, a shopping item, a briefcase.

Faces however can be seen on the street, but vehicles hide their human faces. Vehicles don't have faces of their own. They are expressionless and tell us nothing about the people themselves. A happy face on a human being looks vastly different from an angry face; as a young face does from an old one. Though, the more faces that are found together, the more the individual face become submerged within the mass.

Well, what characterises the individual faces? Hair on a head, no matter about length, or colour, it creates the frame for a personal picture. When meeting other people, what else tells us of them? For instance open, sparkling eyes, how prominent is the nose, if the mouth showing is a dentist's pride, or how well positioned the ears are, will all add to the picture displayed. Finally, the dressing up applied to the face completes the picture.

The cars however own the streets. The hidden faces of their occupants are camouflaged. All that is shown may be the name of personalized number plates, or the colour and model of the choice of car might give some indication of the people. A choice is indicated also if it is a passenger car, ute, truck, motor cycle or bicycle. Mode of transport speaks of work, or leisure.

When traffic and pedestrians move in harmony, the whole show can go on. No faces in the street blur into obscurity, but become proudly part of the streetscape.

Chapter 33

EASTER BUNNY SURPRISE

In 1947, I was 6 years old. Because the time was close to the end of the Second World War, it was a difficult time to celebrate. With spring time approaching in the Northern Hemisphere, regardless of the living conditions young children were wondering what the Eater Bunny had in store for them.

In this year, Easter Sunday still arrived with great expectations. One thing that came with this time was the disappearance of winter and the snow that came with that season. The grass on both sides of the road was now a fresh green, and no longer its brownish colour of winter. Sunlight through a misty, partly cloudy sky called forth a new day.

On this day, I couldn't remain in bed. I wanted to know who the Easter Bunny was visiting, and at the same time, attempt to get a glimpse of him. Mum and Dad were still in bed, so I didn't bother to tell them that I was leaving the house.

The strip of green grass in front of our house almost immediately showed something small which was hidden. I became so excited as I found one red egg, one blue egg, along with one golden-wrapped chocolate rabbit nearby.

I could have easily carried my find into the house, but more was on my mind. Further searching of the surrounding grass failed to reveal any more presents. What about the grass on the other side of the road?

Perhaps there was more to find. How right this was! At first glance many more beautiful presents were half-hidden in the grass. This was starting to look very promising.

What I could manage to carry in my hands, I brought over to the front door of my house. A couple more collection walks to and from the neighbourhood also proved worthwhile. Many more eggs and rabbits, and chocolates were brought to the front door of my house. I was proud, strutting like a rooster, but as it turned out not for much longer.

Mum and Dad had realized that I was no longer in the house. They opened the front door, and wondered why there was such a large Easter Bunny collection waiting there. There were many more presents than what they had helped place in our yard. Surprised or not, they had to ask questions.

"Martin, where did you get all these Easter presents from? We can't remember having seen the Easter Bunny ever carrying so much on his back, just for one child. We think, by the way you look, that you know the answer, don't be afraid, there is nothing to hide, just tell Mum and Dad what happened."

'Well, if you want to know, it's simple. After I checked the lawn in front of our house, and found only a few Easter gifts, I thought I had better check the neighbour's lawn, to see if he had left me some on that side. As you can see, the Easter Bunny thought more of me on the other side of the road.'

Mum and Dad were quick to respond. "Unfortunately it is not that easy. Didn't you think that the children, who live on that side of the road, now cannot find their Easter eggs? You had better put these nice gifts back in their places, where you found them."

Martin did not hesitate to say, 'This is not fair! How do you know these presents are for somebody else?'

"Wait a minute, let's go over to the neighbours and talk to them. Their two young children would have been disappointed without anything from the Easter Bunny."

Just as the group reached the other side of the road, the neighbour's two children realized that something was going on. They came out of their house and started looking for their Easter Bunny presents. Empty handed, they listened to what their neighbours had to say, and the reasons for their visit. Before the talking had started in earnest, little Martin wanted to make his point. 'I was first to find the presents, so shouldn't it be, first find - first keep?'

Martin's parents objected, "first of all, this is not our property, and secondly, we don't want these other children to be unhappy because their gifts have been taken from them. Martin give them back their presents, and you will see how happy you will make them. This way you will become even better friends with one another. Go ahead and pass them back."

With a heavy heart, Martin took several visits over the road to restore the neighbour's Easter Bunny presents. Meanwhile, as their parents had been alerted, they joined in the conversation. They couldn't help but add, 'A nice job has been done to bring everything together. Did Martin help you?'

Martin's parents further explained, "a little misunderstanding took place at first, but in the end everything has turned out fine, and everybody should be happy."

Martin was not that easily convinced, especially as the other two children had the nerve to point out that they were happy someone else had done the work of collecting the Easter gifts for them. Martin couldn't help himself but say, 'what is the reward for my work? You two shouldn't get off so lightly!'

After a silent pause, the parents of the two children said, "You have done well, so early in the morning, to give the Easter Bunny a hand. For that you should receive a reward. How about, one chocolate rabbit and two coloured eggs to add to your Easter Bunny? Our children will happily give these to you. This will settle the issue, and we can all go home and enjoy a nice Easter Sunday."

Chapter 34

MEETING A PARROT

Driving his very own but dilapidated car, the old sea captain was seen along with a most unusual companion. As if it was the most normal thing in the world, next to him was a big, green parrot from the Amazon in Brazil. And this was in Finland, where at that time it was hardly likely to meet any person with such a proud big parrot.

The driver, himself, caught your eye, with his distinctive noble facial features of a sharp pointed nose, a dark full beard all around his face, including moustache. He gave the impression of a seasoned world traveller.

Leaving his country cabin, Petteri went straight towards this new arrival, to welcome and assist the older man to get out of his car. Although his visitor lived in Finland, he spoke to Petteri in the Swedish language. At that time, it was common for someone of Swedish background to also speak Swedish. The Finns had survived under Swedish rule for 700 years, and even though they had not lost their heritage, or their own language, the older generation were just more used to speaking Swedish. The younger generation were less concerned about using the two languages, due to the close proximity of Sweden to Finland.

However, whether Finnish or Swedish, the now gathered children were almost bursting with curiosity. None of them, though, had the courage to go closer to the car, before the bandy-legged sea captain had found solid ground. The parrot meanwhile remained calmly on his seat in the car.

After exchanging a few words with Petteri, the captain moved to the opposite car door, opened it, and spoke to the parrot, using its name 'Laura'. As part of his preparations for removing Laura from the car, the captain took from behind the front seat, one leather glove, which he put directly onto his left hand. The glove not only offered protection for his hand, but also for part of his lower arm.

His next action was to sing, in a crackly voice, a nursery rhyme to the parrot. As soon as he stopped the parrot in turn repeated the melody, surprisingly better than the captain's offering. Only then did Laura move onto the leathered glove.

With his other right hand, the sea captain Johansson caressed the parrot, from under its strong, slightly downward bent beak. This was a signal which meant 'well done, get out of the car now with me'.

Outside the car, Johansson stood erect, holding Laura at eye level. What a magnificent creature this was! Calmly the parrot looked around. Laura had apparently made a satisfactory impact on those present. Arja meanwhile could not restrain herself from curiosity. She could not help but leave the massed children and go closer to parrot Laura, whereby she experienced a real fright. The very sudden, but clear command from the parrot, 'go away!' surprised Arja speechless. Only by repeating the master's nursery rhyme could Laura be convinced to remain on the leather glove next to Arja.

Music was obviously the preferred means of communication. In the end, Arja tried to sing a few more nursery rhyme melodies. Instantly the parrot turned towards her. Laura didn't miss the opportunity to copy-sing Arja's voice, while at the same time making tiny moves towards Arja.

Arja's first reaction was to take a few steps backwards as she couldn't be sure whether she could carry the parrot on her arm without the protection of the leather glove. The powerful claws reminded Arja to be careful, and that her arm was bare. Johansson however had Arja hold her arm alongside his arm, so he could shift in one movement the parrot together with the glove, on to Arja's arm. Now Laura looked with its piercing eyes closely into Arja's. Arja became so excited that she lost all traces of fear. Arja repeated her nursery rhyme, which reassured the parrot, and encouraged Laura to stay. Alternately hopping from one leg to the other seemed to indicate a desire to return to Johansson.

Before the parrot's claws could take a tighter hold on her arm, Arja sang her nursery rhyme more clearly, and indeed Laura seemed to approve. The parrot continued to join in, always improving on the original rhyme which had been voiced by Arja.

The longer Laura remained on Arja's arm the heavier the bird became. As a result, Arja had to support the leather hand, with her other hand propped underneath. This was however in vain, as Laura seemed to disapprove. The bird immediately ceased singing, and instead commenced cawing from deep in its throat.

The moment had arrived for Laura to return to Johansson's arm. This was done as a reverse manoeuvre of before. Peace and silence set in, no talking and no singing. The parrot appeared to have finished with communication, and indeed, did not even as much as flap its wings. They remained flat along the bird's body as if appearing to have forgotten the art of flight. It was as if Laura accepted the change in circumstances, of no longer being in the Amazon forest, and had resigned itself to be compliant with human beings in order to cope.

Arja had certainly experienced great joy with this parrot encounter. She knew quite well that it was unlikely she would ever have such a close meeting with such a beautiful, big and obviously intelligent bird again. According to seaman Johansson, Laura was an aged bird, even compared to the life expectation of humans. Laura was well over one hundred years old. Arja wondered what Laura had in fact thought of the assembled group, as well as the car ride, and the exchange of arms to be seated on.

The car door was gently closed, as the bird resumed its seat, again in the front next to the driver. Arja remained next to the car until Johansson had also re-entered the car; she helped him close his car door. Everyone waved farewell. How Laura felt about proceedings remained contained within the parrot. It was certain though today had been a great change from their daily town routine.

Even many years later, when Arja and her family lived in Brazil, Laura's original homeland, Arja did not come that close to a parrot. Only once, on an occasion in Hawaii did they see a Macao-parrot, but this was in a large fenced area for tourists.

Parrot Laura lived a comfortable life in Finland, with the former sea captain Johansson. During winter, Laura remained in well-heated premises, and when summer returned, Laura's spirits roused, and again the bird answered the melodies of Johansson, in readiness to go out into the warm sunshine of summer.

Unfortunately, it must be mentioned that today, more of these magnificent creatures live in captivity than in their natural rainforest. When will the last 'Laura' be lost from its natural paradise? Nature's rich oases disappear at an alarming scale. Forest readily gives way to the actions of progress.

Laura has let a lasting impression on Arja, even more so than those of Arja's experiences on the species-rich continent of Africa. Arja maintains a lifelong bond with nature, which she has continued with her own family-dorado in tropical Queensland of Australia. Through time and effort, Arja continues to enjoy linking to the natural world.

Chapter 35

TO BE OR NOT TO BE – THAT IS THE QUESTION

(Shakespeare 'Hamlet')

In 1603, Shakespeare stated these words in his play, 'Hamlet'. During this time period, life at court was filled with a high level of social intrigues. What do these words offer us in 2016? Are we still consumed by intrigues for power? One thing is for sure, when we talk about 'to be', our existence is a fact, however 'not to be' opens a completely different set of questions.

If, for some reason, we question our existence, we need to remember that on life's journey, we start with small steps, and for each small step we should be grateful to have come that far, but it is only later life that tells us this.

Wishing yourself or somebody else to 'not be' points to a negative attitude. How far does that get us? It is very difficult to punish yourself, and the words 'not to be' will not simply make it happen. However the words do recognize the struggle humanity has in existing. Life's journey can be overwhelming at times.

A tug of war for power has existed for as long as humans can recall history. Only the methods applied in the struggle have changed. What

400 year earlier was a drama around royalty, is in today's industrial world, across a multi-national field of power brokers.

In Shakespeare's 'Tragical Histories of Hamlet' the playwright looks at revenge, grabs for power, the use of marriage for purpose, and the use of pretences and manipulation, until Hamlet no longer understands the world of his inheritance. Hence the question 'to be or not to be', is the dilemma of knowing who we are and how we fit in.

Today's world, though more complex in its organisation than Hamlet's world, the question 'to be or not to be' remains relevant. Life is no less confusing, or problematic. Enough dramas happen today on all people's doorsteps. We are the actors of our lives, and all we can do, is learn better, how 'to be'.

Chapter 36

JOYFUL WRITING

If we do what we enjoy, we will succeed, and so it is with the joy of writing. In 2016, one would think that not much writing is done by a pen, particularly in a time when computers represent progress, and less work therefore is being done by the pen. But it is still a writer's choice to write a manuscript by hand. Remember, the emphasis is on joy, here. When it comes to presenting the manuscript to an editor, or publisher, there is however, no way around a computer file. To hand in the penned form will only add to early rejection or to a surprising bill.

Once a manuscript is created, it is then that the real fun begins. Rereading, and checking it up to five times is not necessarily extra-special treatment. We are talking here about the author's intentions, to write quality.

When it comes to writing, how much can you learn in the 'how-to department'? The answer is simple: correct writing can be taught, whereas good writing can only be taught to a limited degree. If there is no talent for ideas, creativity or personal experience, there will be no connection to readers through the writing, because a vital link to experiences is missing.

Author Martin Kari has been a member of CWL (Caboolture Writers' Link) for ten years, right from the beginning of the group's organisation. The diversity of the membership is helped by the wise, impartial leadership of Jock Cleeton and assistant Janet Bestmann, to open all minds to writing. How have I, Martin, succeeded with my writing? Since retirement at 65 in 2006, a lot of work has so far gone into my 24 books. The local Caboolture Library has organized some book events for me, and keeps on hand my books for local readers.

A publisher in Melbourne, along with one in New York and one in Frankfurt have also helped me to publish my books in two languages, English and German. These cover a range of writing genres, from a biography, social-political highlights, practical philosophy, travelogues from world adventures, an illustrated children's book, and poetry. (Recently I have won the prestigious 'International Brentano Lyric Award').

Nothing in the end has been guaranteed, nor have surprises been out of the question along the way. Writing one's words, is one thing, whereas selling those words can be quite another.

There is a history behind all writing, which doesn't happen quickly. Everything in life starts small and needs its own time to develop. To make money from writing is short sighted. When money turns up, it's good; when it takes time, it's still good, this issue cannot be forced. Self-publishing can offer alternatives to writing success in some cases.

This is another choice for the writer. The hopeful writer however still cannot go past the importance of personal effort in order to become recognized as a good writer.

BRIEF 'BIO' FOR AUTHOR

Born in 1941 in Transylvania, Martin was educated in Germany, and is now married to a wife from Finland, and has a family of 3 boys and 3 girls, and has had a professional and private life on four continents. He has travelled in many parts of the world, and in 1981 successfully settled in Australia for the last 31 years, on a property in the Caboolture Shire. Martin retired at age 65 in 2006 from the 'professional tread-mill', and reconnected to writing, proving it is never too late to start something new in life. Apart from writing, Martin has learned to present at book events at a local and international level.

Chapter 37

"IF ONLY I HAD KNOWN…"

If we say 'if only I had known', does it mean it is too late to change what has happened? Late or not, let us look at some real life situations, where these words might have been said: The long weekend comes after this Friday. The weather forecast for the coming days is anything but encouraging, with showers and storms predicted. Despite not much hope left for a warm sunny break on the beach, everybody in the factory is in a rush to get out into the weekend.

Michael on the other hand takes his time, allowing he thinks, for the traffic to clear. He believes that the traffic out of the city will slow them all. In order to get home, Michael has to eventually join the exodus of northbound traffic. Though he had waited for the traffic to decrease, it had not happened. Like everyone else, he had been caught up in slow moving cars and he thought to himself that he may well have left in the rush with everyone else from the factory. If only he had known about the traffic snarl.

Finally at home, Michael continued his line of 'if only I had known', because his wife had taken the children to town by bus, and had been unsuccessfully trying to contact him while he had been driving, so they could return home together. 'So what's next?' Michael asked himself. Finally he concluded that the opposite direction into town must surely be less busy, therefore returning to town would be less hassle to collect his family, and only cost him a little time and some fuel.

The entire family is finally returned home, in time to hear the six o'clock news and weather. Michael hears no mention of the impending rain previously forecast for the long weekend. Instead sunshine is promised. What confusion! 'If only I had known that the forecast had changed, we could have better planned our short holiday at the beach.'

All that can be done now is to have a good night's sleep, and discover whether it is rain or shine on Saturday. In fact, thunder and rain visits in the middle of the night, and clears to a blue, cloudless sky in the morning, where the sun reigns unopposed. So the forecast had not been entirely wrong, just a little out on the time frame.

AUTHOR'S NOTE

'If only I had known how much work goes into writing I ….' Doesn't it show that even behind an uncertainty, a positive outcome can emerge? We only have to be persistent in what we pursue.

Looking for excuses like 'if only I had known' is not helpful. Excuses accompany us persistently in life, with the next excuse seemingly just around the corner. We should realize that to know everything is impossible. This is why we err. If we linger over something that lies behind us, it only puts the brakes on to moving forwards in life. Better to change direction at the time, and not allow blinkered vision to control our actions.

From the misjudgement of 'if only I had known', we can learn flexibility to gain a better life. Life will go on and that is reason enough to keep going, and to leave the thought 'if only' behind.

Chapter 38

THE POSTMAN

Already the morning hours have advanced close to midday. Helen takes a break from home duties, while husband Michael continues to work in a factory in the nearby large city. Their two children are at school and life appears to running its usual course.

Helen decides to check the mailbox, and see what the postman has left for them. The dogs stay behind in the house yard, not going to the gate entry with her. The timing for the postman to show up on his bicycle is very nearly exactly to the minute of his arrival. And so it happens on this day.

'How is your day going?' is exchanged in welcome between Helen and the postman. The day is full of sunshine, and Helen further inquires 'what good news do you have for us today? Hopefully no bills today, if you know what I mean,' she states.

With a smile, the postman answers "whether postman or not we all have to deal with the bills. But there are other things that the post can deliver which brings enjoyment. We are also here to keep people in touch, even over long distances. Well I better keep moving, have a nice day."

'Thanks for your friendly service,' Helen says to him, as he leaves to make his way to next door.

Years later, how has the delivery of mail changed? First of all, in a time of equal rights, delivery is more likely in a van, driven by a post woman. Time has become money, so the certainty of time of delivery is not available, Helen never knows on which day the post will arrive. At least she tries to understand the economical side. What she has difficulty in comprehending is the lack of personal exchanges between the delivery driver and the receiver of the post. No time for social interaction, for deliveries must be timely and efficient. Then, of course, everything is now high-tech, and really there is no-one there to talk to. Helen and her family ask themselves if the sacrifice of human contact for progress is worthwhile.

Hopefully, as time progresses we will find other ways to connect with the people in our world.

SMOKING SCHOOL DISCIPLINE

School discipline has always been a challenge, even in times past. Not all students are angels, and usually it is only a small number of students who choose to fool around. So it happened during my school years, that one day during a lunch break, outside the school premises two male students calmly pulled a cigarette out and started to puff away. This was as they had seen adults do, though these boys were in the company of some other students.

My friend and I saw a female teacher coming our way in a hurry. There was no time to warn our fellow students to hide their cigarettes. Instead, the teacher found herself suddenly in the middle of a cloud of cigarette smoke, blowing into her face.

Such behaviour was of course not tolerated even outside the school grounds, as it was still during school hours, and in proximity to the school. At the time, however, parents were able to identify by letter, if their students were allowed to smoke, but if this notification hadn't happened, the students would clearly be expelled from school.

This time, though, the situation was settled without too severe repercussions for the offending students. As a first offence, a warning was given, along with an understanding that because of their youth, fooling around was part of their growing up. At this time it seemed easier to understand and leave these slip-ups behind, than carry a school exclusion into adulthood.

Chapter 40

FATHER'S GOOD NIGHT STORIES

I recall an event related to my father-in-law's goodnight storytelling, which was related to me by my wife. It has remained especially firm in my memory. The story itself involved two young stowaways who wanted to see the world and its different, marvellous countries; unnoticed and free of charge.

> 'The two young boys met up at school and set about to follow a dream; a dream of how to see the world and its many wonderful creatures and countries.
>
> What they knew so far was that ships visited many countries by sea. The boys didn't talk to anyone else about their plans, and agreed one night to secretly leave their beds, sneak out and meet half-way between their homes. As they did not live far from one another, this was a good plan.
>
> The moon shone clearly in the sky, and the light helped the two boys to make their way to the harbour. One large ship at the quay attracted their attention. Both boys believed that this ship would go as far as they wanted to go.

Fortunately, the jetty and the gangway on to the ship was unattended, so they slipped unseen on to the ship, and made their way inside, where light and only a few people who were little interested in the two would-be passengers, greeted them. The ship was about to set its sails for departure to the open ocean. The whole ship moved gently forwards and backwards, as well as from side to side.

On the ship, the day is very different from a day on land at home. There is much on offer on board a ship; things to look at, everywhere a helping hand is welcome; there is regular 'yummy' dinner from the kitchen, as well as a night's sleep in a swing.

First Africa turns up with brilliant sunshine, and heat out of a clear sky. As soon as the ship docks, giraffes with their long necks reach on to the ship's deck, welcoming the travellers in the African way. Not long after, on one side of the road leading into an African town elephants wait in line swinging their trunks, whereas on the opposite roadside, lions majestically show the new arrivals, their respect.

Closer into the city, chimpanzees jump freely across the road, holding bananas in their paws, to show what they like to eat best. Even the air is filled with songs from colourful birds, both small and large. Butterflies and beetles compete with their colours, crossing their pathways skilfully. This must be paradise the two young explorers think. Time ashore goes by much more quickly than at home, because of all these new encounters. The ship's journey however has to continue, if they want to see more of the world.'

This night-time story however, had prompted two friends from the same neighbourhood to 'pilgrim' all the way to the city's harbour where the police, alerted by the stowaways' parents, collected them near to a docked ship. Fortunately, this was just in time before the children's plan to secretly board ship could turn into reality.

Luckily also, once the errant duo arrived in front of the monstrous ship's hull, they could not pluck up the courage to board the monster.

In the end, it was a return trip home in the police car for the runaways, which was not quite so distant or adventurous as they had dreamed. Sometimes an idea can spark an action in anyone, regardless of their age, especially when their fantasies lack vital reality experience. Nothing is lost, if at the end, all turns out all right, even if it's a young dream excursion.

Nobody in the neighbourhood could be upset when the police returned the young would-be world travellers safely to their doorsteps.

Upon hearing about the incident, Petteri, my wife's father, was amused, promising from then on he would try to tell less adventurous good-night stories. The story telling father continued to entertain the children, both close-by and in the wider neighbourhood, however this time not with a story, but with and extraordinary adventure.

> *Nobody could guess who was behind where the military tank showed up, on a local street in the middle of a perfectly warm, sunny summer day. Incredibly, the story teller was behind its wheel, and offering to take a group of neighbourhood children in and on top of the tank, for a joy ride through the centre of the town. While the adventure-party boisterously went on, people in the town's centre thought war had broken out.*
>
> *Police stepped in bringing the party to a stop. No bad blood was caused, and the fun had not even been spoiled by the officials. The police offered to give the children a lift back home, just not in the tank this time.*

Chapter 41

"DON'T PLAY WITH THE MUCKY PUPS."

Even though not born in Ettlingen, I spent my youth there, and I think often of this town even though I now live in far distant lands. The surrounding hills of the Black Forest haven't moved from their original position, and they still look gently and benevolently over the town. Time has not changed the physical landmarks of the town, objects such as the churches, the town hall and the town's castle remain as they once were. For how long into the future these well-known landmarks will remain is uncertain. Changes due to progress are gradual, and there are always those who are ready to move on.

The expansive views of the city from the Bismark Tower embrace the landscape, becoming lost in the plains towards the main river Father Rhein, allowing its much smaller tributary the river Alb to break through its narrow valley. From the surrounding Black Forest water still runs in a leisurely fashion through the old and new parts of the town. Its current not only decorates the surrounding countryside, but it also talks quietly to people – burbling along for quite some time to sparsely as well as densely populated areas of activity along its course. Like the course of the river, everything ebbs and flows in our lives.

Contrary to a river course, our ways in life do not run in defined directions. Our memory mostly tells us from where we have come. As a visitor returning to Ettlingen, my memory is jolted back to the past, and I wonder who of the current citizens shares these same memories.

My remembrances start in the heart of the city, there, where the tributary of the Alb joins its original riverbed course. Sixty-five years earlier the inner city's cobble stone streets were made for its pedestrians. Then, only a few cars were about.

The children at that time, had local playgrounds available, one of which was located at the confluence of the river Alb. Children, especially in summer, went for a swim here. This happened from the road stonewalls, lower river banks and often with the help of hand-made wooden rafts. In those days we were referred to as 'mucky pups'.

During my visit to Ettlingen, one of these 'mucky pups' recognized me from his luxury car window, as I walked around town. He stopped, addressed me by name and invited me into his limousine, with the intention of giving me a lift to my parent's address in Schöllbronner Street.

In all the years since our rascal pranks together, he had become a self-educated man, with a family, and in a position of Technical Director of a worldwide Technical Development Company. He too had learnt valuable life lessons which had assisted him to advance respectfully in his life. He was a contrast to the number of people I have met, who though having followed an educational path, have never become active with their knowledge.

One particular lesson out of the school of life brutally caught up with the Alb Street gang, when Hämmerle, the younger brother of Hamm fell victim to a serious infection. It was obviously from the polluted water of the river Alb. Consequently swimming in the local river became officially prohibited.

The river Alb had to undergo a substantial cleansing process for a number of years. Before this, fish were not even seen in its water. The local factories, particularly the Buhl and Ettlingen Maxau, plus the chemical laundry called Bardusch were obliged to return their used water only when sufficiently cleaned, into the river. In the beginning of the new millennium, people now can look into the clear and safe water of the Alb.

During the 1950's, carnivals took place in the town, but these have fallen out of favour through the following years. At one time, I could remember groups of young people, dressed up as cowboys and Indians, moving through the town. These children were recruited from the local schools, sport's organisations, as well as the boy scouts, and junior fire brigade to advertise these associations during the carnival parade, along with a host of other business organisations.

During one year's event, a type of battle took place on the building site of the new autobahn to the west of the town. There was no real explanation for the conflict, except that there were rumours of course of what had occurred. It presumably started with the carnival 'fools' being called to assemble around a large fire pit. From outside of town, a group of trouble makers, armed with some even on horseback, supposedly planning on taking over the peaceful carnival gathering. Police were called in to put a stop to this potentially dangerous encounter.

From this time on, only the official carnival parade was allowed to go ahead. This was unfortunate, as previously the carnival-fools had moved freely throughout the town, advertising various organisations.

The first school I visited on return to Ettlingen was the Thibaut School. I still remember quite well, my class teacher Mr Furrer. The cane was used at the time to deal with disobedient students, with the aim of making them into good citizens. Sometimes the cane was interfered with by students, who would quietly slice length-cuts into the cane so that when the teacher used it, it would fly into small pieces, distracting the teacher from his mission. Then, detention would be given as an alternative discipline measure, where students were given time to think about their actions.

At primary school, from year 4 onwards English was part of the lesson program. At the time this received some negative attention as it was believed that Secondary school should be officially responsible and not Primary school, so the lessons were rejected shortly after they had been introduced. At the same time, there were school trials for varying the start of the school year, either spring time or autumn. Here, the Ministry of Education left its mark.

Today the Town Hall still stands in the neighbourhood of the Thibaut School. Sixty years ago, the Hall had a barrel-like facade, which represented a classical 'Biedermeier-stile'. Artistic ornates were embellished on both the inside and the outside. Contrary to this, the renovated Hall today represents a simple straight forward architectural style.

To continue on from Primary school, was to attend Secondary school, at the parents' expense. This school was located within the former monastery buildings of the Herz-Jesu Church. Only in later years did school attendance become free of charge.

In 1957, new secondary school facilities became available in Schiller Street. A variety of teachers, under the leadership of School Directors, Mr Bissinger and later on Mr Suhr, tried their best with student Martin (author). Even though this writer felt he had not gained much from his learning, more had penetrated than had originally been apparent. Hair pulling and ear-boxing both at home and at school, allowed my 'hard iron' to become properly forged.

Comments from teachers of the time, stated:

Mrs Zollner, Latin:	*I still believe you could have done better.*
Mr Watzke, Math:	*The solution must be tickled out.*
Mrs Kesenheimer, German:	*Nothing leads to nothing.*

Mr Borger, Math/Biology:	*Martin, you'll soon get a hiding on your ear lobe.*
Mrs Wetz, French:	*I need to have a look at home.*
Mr Weh, Music:	*Immature gang, which you are.*
Mr Kirsch, Sports:	*Latin excellent, for sports you better start cutting wood first.*
Mr Koch, Arts:	*This is still far away from art.*
Mr Stenzel, Deutsch:	*The play reveals the language to us.*
Mr FuEnglish:	*Next time you better get it into your heads*

As a student of this time, I was happy enough to go as far as Intermediate school. The high-tech company of Argus in my neighbourhood accepted my application for apprentice toolmaker. From here on, my life-learning commenced. I did so well initially, that my apprentice time was shortened, as well as being offered the 'Federal Price' for my final toolmaker certificate. This didn't happen without insistence from all involved. The apprentice master Mr Schindler had proven from day 1 that he would say things only once. On the first day, new apprentices were given instructions as to how to respectfully handle measuring instruments. For me, it was a disaster, as I dropped a vernier. The master's clip on the ear, and prompt 'you don't do that again!' was all I needed for my time as an apprentice. I never dropped my vernier again.

The trade and industry teachers of the vocational school were keen to impress apprentices with newly emerging knowledge for one day per week. One teacher in particular saw beyond the existing capabilities of his students, and mentored this writer in a writing competition, the topic of which was 'Democracy and Communism in comparison'.

Former Bundespräsident Theodor Heuss recognised student Martin with a book prize for his outstanding efforts. My writing had drawn on my travel experiences into East Berlin, in 1961. This was very shortly before the Berlin Wall separated West and East. From firsthand knowledge, my travelling companion, Frank Sauer and I had experienced the impact of communism on one part of a society, while the other half of the society became westernized.

My training company were very proud of my success, and the company director, Mr Bierbaum, consequently invited me to also write a suitable report about the company, Argus. The local newspaper had also supported my writing efforts at constructive criticism, by stating 'where there is no balanced criticism, there is no progress'.

Meanwhile decades have gone past, before the leading ideas of my time in Ettlingen have shown me as an internationally recognized author. Not only had plenty of water run in the local river Alb, but to become a world citizen Martin had worked and lived with his family, on four continents Much formal learning also took pace outside of Ettlingen: a correspondence course in engineering to parallel the apprenticeship, abitur at Karlsruhe, a night grammar school, student of the university Ruperto Carola in Heidelberg, plus various expeditions into the world Finally came partnership with wife Arja, raising a family of six children, experiencing life in different continents and establishing a settled home base in Australia, in 1981.

To once more return to Ettlingen and this time to share the experiences with my daughter Gucki would be most pleasing. Gucki, who studied at the University of Darwin, and is currently teaching music there, has surpassed my guitar abilities. Gucki performing in the wonderful Asam Hall of the Ettlingen castle would become a dream come true for the town's music lovers. She performes outstanding guitar interpretations of classical works, using composers such as Bach, Giuliani, Sors, Villa Lobos, Barrios, Pujol, Lauro, Brouwer, Albeniz and others.

This would be an opportunity for the new citizens of Ettlingen to experience the musical talent of one of its offspring from far off 'Down Under'. What a special occasion to hear masterful classical guitar music in their Asam Hall.

I could not but reflect on my time learning music at the conservatory Karlsruhe. My love for music was obvious, but home inevitably applied the brakes. 'Don't get too involved with something that can help your future very little' were the words of home. In retrospect, perhaps this was not all bad advice.

Another local circle for music, 60 years ago was the German Boy Scout Confederation under the patronage of the industrialist Theo Zurstrassen. Over time, this positive, meaningful youth activity experienced financial cuts. Friendships from that time though, have lasted to present time, even over the distance to Australia. The words from Ettlingen 'to go out into the world' have been honoured. I was not alone to venture forth, emerging from the small cell of Ettlingen into world citizenship.

When it came to sport, TSV-Ettlingen's active executive committee were influential. Their sport's personality, Mr Kary, left marks of significance over the decades. Professionally, Mr Kary was a sales person for the local brewery Huttenkreuz. Mr Kary proved decisive in providing alternative therapies for this writer's lasting personal health issues as part of recovering from a broken spine.

As a result of Mr Kary's community and educational work, our own sport stadium, located in the south of town was built. Until Mr Kary, this had been a slow moving project, but on his arrival, and using his motto 'practical men act on their own', the sport's complex became a reality in less than three years. He organised all sport's members to be on hand, late on weekdays, and full steam ahead on weekends.

We all achieved good personal results in all disciplines, from athletics to gymnastics. I still remember our champion in gymnastics, Bär, who emerged from the club's efforts. Mr Kary remained a shining example of physical education for the TSV club in Ettlingen, over the decades.

On my return to the town, I came across Mr Kary at the now very modern indoor swimming pool in Luisen Street. Although now of advanced years, he had refused to accept the signs of an aging body. Out of the sport's equipment room (often referred to as the torture chamber) he emerged, entering the pool room. He presented as a good looking athletically built man who retained his youthful body, and his sprightliness because of his sport's activities. He recognised me as if we regularly saw one another. Given my age at the time was 72, I could only be in awe of his example, I was reminded of the wise testimonial: 'Mens sana in corpore sano' (only in a healthy body, a healthy mind is at home). It is out of laziness we pay little attention to such demands, until we experience the down-sides to it.

Much lives in my memories about Ettlingen. The past can teach us much for the future. Here in 2013 how does Ettlingen stand? Talking with the citizens, I learn that there are not many original citizens left. Why is this so? One thing I observed on my visit is the number of people sitting and dining in the inner-city's cobble streets, during week days. Fifty years ago this would not have happened. Then Ettlingen was a rich city with much industry and places for work, such as Lorenz, Argus, Etllingen Maxau, Buhl and Elba. No trace of them is left today. How many work sites are now offered to its citizens? This kind of 'progress' has even made it to Australia.

At least the churches of Ettlingen remain in the same place. However it remains to be seen if the custom of transforming them into inner-climbing and exercise places as has happened in other locations in Germany, occurs. Isn't this inappropriate to attracting church visitors?

Progress is good, but it should not be at the expense of the history of the establishment.

My visit to Ettlingen has concluded, and my destination is again back to 'Down Under', Australia. I will continue to enjoy my memories of both past and present Ettlingen, a town I once knew so very well.

Chapter 42

LOVE IS NOT ONLY A WORD

Love is a peculiar game
It goes from person to person,
A ball played with unwritten rules,
Catching only the open player
Not with its great variety,
Because limits apply also here,
To follow the rules for the single and all.

Sometimes a coincidence can help,
Another time it is poor luck or intention,
when hope allows this game.
All gates and doors are open for
possibilities,

Be it committed, spoken or not,
Love too lives in the present
From the past, up to a hopeful future,
Where life is not hanging by a thread,
Still going through the ups and downs of
Life,
Granting strength with, without
possessions

Even when put to the real test,
Love lasts in the end longer
Than anything else in life,
Until we finally depart this world.

Love lives with us,
Only it can survive us,
There, where its diverse threads
With sympathy, consideration, devotion
Allow life to move on.

(words, Martin Kari, 2016)

Chapter 43

SWIMMING LESSONS

Swimming lessons were once a sport's subject at school. In Finland, the Turku-town indoor pool allowed the public in on alternate days; one day was designated for male swimmers and one day for female swimmers. This may seem peculiar, however in typically Finnish cultural fashion swimming took place without bathing suits, just simply naturally naked.

Some young people, like the author's Finnish wife, held some reservations about naked swimming in the company of strangers.

To avoid swimming lessons however required a letter from home, which meant that though an exemption would be granted, this usually meant an exchange lesson was given for another replacement task. For example, a 'lesson' might be recording old grave stones in the local cemetery, and tidying up and weeding the grave site to improve the look of the area.

The substitute activity was not exactly popular, and often lead to arrangements between classmates, who would exchange grave stone notes with free time away from school. In hindsight students didn't really know whether the teachers were aware of what was happening, or whether they turned a blind eye to who was really down for cemetery duty. At least the practice seemed ignored so long as students stayed under the radar.

During female swimming lessons, there were certain girls who would comment on the appearance of other female students. This was hard, given the sensitive nature of those with developing bodies, and their co-existing lack of self-confidence. Comments like: 'your boobs look rather hungry', or, 'you have missed out with your front and back; your hair has been visited by mice; you…a good swimmer, that's a joke; no wonder you have no friends so far; rather look at yourself, you are only bones, missing meat in the right places,' and so on.

Such undercover taunting, which came and went, depending on the girls, helped at least to teach the targeted students to ignore such remarks, and to find their strength to rise above the ridicule. We all have to learn how to deal with such challenges, and to develop a strong personality able to withstand life's negatives. Both Arja and I have attempted in life to accept difficulties as they come along, and to learn to be stronger than them.

Chapter 44

FINLAND AND ALEKIS KIVI

Let me give you, the reader, some information of historical Finnish facts that have assisted the birth of a nation. Many people of today's Finland often take for granted the sacrifices of their forefathers, that allow them to live comfortably today.

Aleksis Kivi is recognized as the father of the Finnish language, despite Michael Agricola who established the first Finnish ABC-book, and translated the bible's New Testament into Finnish. Kivi had founded the Finnish language almost three hundred years earlier.

Together both Swedish and Finnish as a spoken language, mainly survived with the peasants, who were mostly illiterate. It developed that Finnish became regarded as a language of the lower classes, in comparison Swedish became the declared official language, across Sweden and Finland in 1883.

After the Finnish declaration of independence in 1917, a question of identity flared during the civil war of 1917 – 1919. One political side in Finland wanted to join the Bolsheviks of Russia, calling themselves the 'Reds', while others, 'the Whites' opted for an independent Finland. Both sides however stood for the use of the Finnish language, with a decision made to adopt Finnish as the language of Finland.

Mostly it had been the peasants who had preserved the Finnish identity. Most of these could only lease land from higher ranking members of society, right up until the beginning of the twentieth century. Here, the language has played a vital role in preserving Finnish identity, surviving with the majority of its population – the peasant 'underdogs'. Thus the Finnish language has retained currency, and not been subsumed by the direction of the 'higher ranks'.

Chapter 45

FRANKFURT BOOK FAIR - 2012

On invitation from the Frankfurter Publishers, author Martin Kari attended the Frankfurt Book Fair, for the first time, in October, 2012. There, the author was given the opportunity to present himself and his most recent novel, 'Underdog Comedies', (German edition 'Unterm Scheffel Komödien') at the publisher's exhibition stand.

A great number of visitors attended over the five allocated days. Curious onlookers, hobby readers, officials, business people from the international book markets, and representatives of the press took the opportunity to attend talks, and question times with the author. This was well-supported by the publisher's personnel who were keen to express their interest in the new literature.

My book talk was clearly listed on the fair's calendar of events, as well as receiving a two page book review in the publisher's Literature Magazine. At the same time the local newspaper of my hometown of Ettlingen presented a complex report, including photo, of its former citizen. Following on from the fair, there was to be also, a presentation at the 'Book Vienna' in November, then another presentation at 'Book London' in England, and 'Book Leipzig' in March the next year.

My German edition of the book was published first, with the English translation to follow shortly after. This was just what happened, and did not reflect on any value judgements made at the time.

My book holds up to the mirror ten different professions. What do the professions of king, beggar, doctor, teacher, plumber and others find out as they look at their reflections? Why, that we are all 'underdogs' of somebody else. In my book, everybody has a commentary that is why the book's style changes from character to character enriching the drama with valuable reading material.

As a result of my German contacts, a theatre group has also expressed interest in my work for their short-play-programme. How this will be appraised remains to be seen. Ideas with imagination are the foundations for all writing. I have partly followed in the footsteps of the French dramatist, Moliere, who even in the seventeenth century applied criticism to his own society in his comedies.

Criticism does not disallow progress. If criticism can find a smile in a comedy, this can only be regarded as useful. The ones, who maintain a smile in their lives, are more likely to enjoy a longer life, i.e. those who smile, live longer. Criticism is also more palatable when presented humorously.

On my trip to Frankfurt, from Australia, I certainly did not forget to pack my smile, no matter how busy. I was only one of the 800 passengers on the huge new A380 aircraft, from Singapore to Frankfurt, return. My first flight on this technical wonder-creation was most comfortable. However, given the great distance, the time difference, and the opposite seasons of the year from Australia to my destination, the flight still takes its toll. No-one can claim to arrive well rested, and ready to go.

I stayed in the city of Kassel, to the north of Frankfurt, with a good friend, so it felt like home. From here I commuted daily via a high speed train for the 5 day event, held at an impressive high-rise exhibition tower.

Every day, during the exhibition, masses of visitors pushed their way through the numerous buildings. It seemed that people had no choice either to be sucked in or being pushed along, because it was so crowded. I spent most of my time at my publisher's exhibition stand in order to keep up with the numerous enquiries. The event catered to well-known authors, and publishers. All were to be seen here. The event has the reputation as well of greatly assisting aspiring authors.

In 2013 the country of New Zealand was the guest of honour. This country is a strong ally and neighbour of Australia. They drew attention to themselves by performing their 'Hakka' from the very beginning of the event. This country was well-presented by its' authors, whereas Australia had a much smaller contingent, of whom I was one.

Despite the great number of visitors over the five days, the 'Damocles Sword' hanging over the book-world couldn't be denied. Our digital technology brings not only progress, but it also forces publishers to adapt their way of publishing. The book market is changing rapidly and, whether one likes it or not, it is shrinking. Co-responsible for these developments are: E-books, self-publishing, tablets, internet accessibility and fewer readers within the younger generation. These have become new challenges for the publishing industry worldwide.

It is difficult to predict clearly, how books will be regarded in the future. In the end, however, only the better and stronger will survive. As an author I must commit to producing my very best writing, to communicate effectively with others, and to avoid following the trends as suggested by writing fashion. It is commonly known that trends come and go, even in the world of books.

Each author must determine for his/herself where he/she stands not only in the present, but for future directions. Nothing is new when it comes to tackling difficulties. As writers and publishers we will all share in the challenge. Hopefully, 'all is well that ends well' to quote Shakespeare. In this sense, the close of the Frankfurt Book Fair for my publisher and I was a celebration of a successful 25 year connection, to which a classical music concert provided the backdrop.

Having now returned to Australia, I can reflect that the Book Fair opened my understanding of my own writing and the reception into international literature requirements. Now, I am regarded as both an Australian, as well as a German author, which is enough to be proud of. I have been invited to further book fairs, and in 2014, I presented my book talk as a special feature in five languages (German, English, French, Portuguese and Finnish). 2014 was also the year that Finland was the guest of honour.

In addition, German Literature Television aired my contribution to the world of words. Worth noting is that besides the usual sources of bookshops for words, internet providers including the German National Bibliotheca, including notes with the 'German Association of Authors', as well as the National Australian Library, and Australian State Libraries keep my books for future generations.

It is important to understand; in writing there are plenty of small well-considered steps which are the key to success. How long will success last? Not even the stars could deliver that answer. In a thousand years much of today will not matter. What matters is the good that is achieved today.

Chapter 46

MY BOOK FAIR PRESENTATION

What is suggested here is how an author's book presentation can spark general interest not only for the book but also for the International Book Fair – Frankfurt. Such an event demands the ability to address an international audience, in such a way as to convey one's words in an easy, but interesting manner. I have experienced many authors who have had difficulty with the speaking component. Here, I leave it to the reader to gauge my performance of this task. What follows, is a sample of one of three speeches covering three different books, over a three year period.

'My name is Martin Kari, and I have just arrived from Queensland, the Sunshine State of north-eastern Australia. I am here to present my book *Underdog Comedies* published by the Frankfurt Publishing Group. The German version of this book, *Unterm Scheffel Komödien* was launched last year, at this International Fair. Both books reflect the same story, but use the idiomatic differences of the two languages. Both have been separately written. Neither is a translation of the other.

Having lived and worked on four continents, I have also taken on board more languages post-school. This enables me to express my thoughts therefore, in more than one language. With regards to

Australia, you will be interested to learn that 70 languages besides the official English are spoken in this newly emerging society.

My welcome to you is in English, for it gives me great pleasure to also welcome those visitors today, from an English speaking background.

(In French): Mesdames et messieurs soyez le bienvenue à la presentation d'une satire modern en deux languages.

(In Finnish- because my wife is from Finland, and I honour her and our friends present today) :

Toivottan myös tervetulleeksi hyvät suomalaiset ystävät.

As the Book Fair's guest of honour is Brazil this year, I also welcome this country in their own Portuguese language : *Bom dias senhores e senhoras durante la Feira De Livros em Frankfurt. Eo dar as boas vindas a todos os Brasilieros tambem.*

<u>Continuing in English</u>:

Today is Sunday, the 13th day of the month, let us hope that all goes well for us, fingers crossed for me, 'August von Goethe Lieraturverlag' has decided to make my book available to English readers.

Let me introduce my book, 'Underdog Comedies' to you.

How far are we prepared to acknowledge that we are 'glasshouse-mates'? There is one main rule for people in glasshouses, they shouldn't throw stones! This means think carefully about your comments about others as your words may indeed apply to yourself.

Allow me to state that it is humanity's progress which has brought changes to our intellect and our performance. Glasshouse-mates are increasingly challenged from the outside. Not many escape the underdog-role from either inside or outside these houses. There is always someone who influences our actions, or who will sit in judgement of them.

As an independent reader has already stated, 'This is Martin Kari at his thought-provoking best! He offers, as always, some challenging ideas for us to read about and think about. His characters come alive......' (Joane Morish, Bachelor of Arts University of Queensland/Australia).

As a taste of the book, to aid further understanding here is a brief outline of contents:

Chapter 1   ROYALTY
              Looking behind the scene/p14
              A court jester "Chewing Gum", offers distraction/p16

Chapter 2   OUR NOTORIOUS SOCIAL LADDER
              Where do we commonly see the so called beggar?
              Our beggar welcomes a new day/p37
              Beggar at work/p41
              Beggar is also somebody else/p112

Chapter 4   THE DENTIST
              The dentist in people's eyes/p109
              The dentist at work/p112

Having chosen the daily life of professionals, my book also touches on the life of a surgeon, and a task performed by the Royal Flying Doctor Service in Outback Australia.

I also pay attention to toolmakers, plumbers, teachers, mechanics and garbage collectors. I let each one out of his/her glasshouse, so they can experience – we are all underdogs.

FINAL WORDS

When something is at its best, we should not forget how to get to an end. I wish to thank you for your attention. I wish for you to take from my book the serious observations as well as the fun given in my words, into your daily lives.

Remember the book is now available in two languages. I encourage you to make a book purchase, in the language that most suits you.

At least at the end, it should be all smiles, if not you can't be helped, however still enjoy your Sunday. Goodbye, auf Wiedersehen, au revoir ja näkemiin.

Chapter 47

WHO WOULD HAVE THOUGHT...

…….that this could happen, or not? Why is this so?
Questions usually arrive more quickly than answers can
be found. What has real life to say about this?

Politics for instance has never been an accidental issue that is discussed. Before an election, many would-be representatives emerge to announce 'heaven on earth' in their promises. As elections operate on their own schedule, it is in the outcomes where voters experience the intensity of offered concessions, or spoken promises for a better future. When finally it comes to the election, it is only in the aftermath that a clear picture emerges. No matter even with the best of will, human actions seem to differ from the promises. 'Who would have thought this' often remains the question.

Further general public conversations will also include the topic of the weather. As we all like the sunshine, we attach our hopes to seeing it on a daily basis. What, however, the weather bureau announces, may not be sunshine every day. If we believe the forecasts, and plan accordingly, then disappointment is also waiting for us. When the sunshine has been driven out by rain and wind, then we can ask ourselves, who would have thought this.

Spinning this yarn further, hope remains a bridge-builder in life. At the outset not everything is obvious each time. The crack of the whip is known to happen at its end, and this often is the only outcome we can truly see. For example, when a skilled hand hammers a nail into a wall, we may also see an accidental hit to the thumb – a one off, but certainly not expected, or hoped for.

Similarly, with hope a young man is granted permission to go ahead with pilot training, even though his parents are too terrified to board an aircraft. Hope drives a positive outcome in this situation.

Regardless of the outcome, we all experience surprises on a daily basis. On one occasion it may be a less pleasant outcome; at another time it may be a really pleasant one. We learn that regardless of ups and downs, life continues anyway. Confidence and courage help us find the answer to the question, who would have thought this?

Chapter 48

THE GIRL WHO RAN FROM...

We all need advice and a little help in life from time to time. The girl who ran away from home is really a wake-up-call to everyone. Since we have allowed more freedom of expression to enter society, we have also had to accept the consequences out of this increased freedom.

If for instance you have children, you are guaranteed some surprises as you raise them. A few of these surprises, which are not too out of the ordinary, are put to paper here. Criticisms that go 'you don't live in this world anymore'; or, 'you are as old as Methuselah and have forgotten to enjoy life', or, 'I don't work my guts out, what for and for whom?' To these and much more, parents have to listen sometimes as their child makes up their mind about the state of affairs of their home life. Forming their own opinions, is part of developing the intellect, and it is comforting to think that when emotions go up, they will also come down again.

Such outbursts occur usually out of the blue. Why is that so? So many class mates and others who live in town appear to live life differently from what the young person is told at home. Who is right or wrong? The outside world seems to encourage a freer life, but too often there is no regard for the consequences. Life teaches us all, sooner or later that without effort we cannot expect much.

The 'old' days are gone when family life was less challenged by hard-done-by adolescents. Discipline has been widely declared as old-fashioned. The purpose of family is to prepare offspring for independence, and allowing them to go out into the world unharmed. Advice seems to fall on the deaf ears of the young. Time is in short supply. When aiming for something, everyone has to learn the need to give themselves time. When the answer comes from outside of the home, it is so much easier to follow. Rarely, is it asked, who is supporting this?

Parents may find some comfort in the fact that conflict when raising the young is as old as humanity. Where there is progress, it is inevitable that someone will be left behind. The more this happens, so can individuals within a family, drift apart. Therefore, the focus has to be on inclusive progress, where all can keep up, and parents are not isolated from their children.

In most cases, parents care about their offspring's fate and do not wish their children to run away from home. This means parents need to stay in tune with their children. Extended family, good friends and to a certain extent the community authorities all face the task of establishing effective communication.

Everything depends on how much each side have dug their heels in, and refuse to move. To achieve a mutual understanding, needs an ability to step back from one's own point of view to understand firstly the views of others, then to allow a new, better start point for re-establishing relations.

Pointing the finger towards an assumed wrong side, will only deepen the rift between youth and adults. It is better to listen, and be observant of each other, with a view to reducing conflict, so that a daughter does not make the choice of running away from home.

Chapter 49 / A

THE HAND OF FAITH – PART 1

(poem-form)

Many hands make much possible ;
And where do these hands come from?
Two hands we can claim our own,
Every other hand should be beneficial
As long as faith accompanies it.
And what does a faith-hand looks like?

A hand usually is visible for us
And what about the hand of faith ?
Has anybody ever seen this hand ?
If not, how come ?
Does the invisible still exists,
When it comes to lending a helping hand ?

All we do, hope, achieve, even fail
Is carried by faith invisibly too,
When answers don't reach us anymore.
All is left, is faith in ourselves,
Trusted to your next of kin, a friend,
Restoring confidence to carry on.

Words can become a supporting hand,
They need to be chosen carefully,
Not to disrupt the path to faith.
Action too can support and undermine,
Depending much on a timing,
Where a will finds an open door.

The opponents of a hand of faith
Also rise invisibly from obscurity,
Recruiting lies, deception, fake, fraud,
Which only suppress in a trial of strength
A good will of many a hands,
Including the hand of faith.

No matter what happens, faith is crucial
In any circumstances of a daily life,
Even love depends on the hand of faith,
Because where is no faith, there is no love.
And how much derives from love,
Gives us the understanding of faith.

Chapter 49 / B

THE HAND OF FAITH – PART 2

(story-telling form)

'Where did you hang around for almost half of last night?' These are the parent's words as he confronts his son, unsuccessfully attempting to enter the house, very late, through the garage side door. The answer often requires a 'hand of faith' or belief from the family. Belief which will set aside inconveniences, fear, and misunderstandings.

One small further example: a post office customer requests assistance from a near-by employee, to manage the self-service equipment. The queue in front of the regular service desk is too long for the customer to join, but he is unsure of what to do, when bill paying at the self-serve. The employee is happy to help.

And indeed, the equipment delivers a receipt after accepting the money tendered. The coin change is taken from the return bowl and passed into the customer's hands. A thank you is offered, and the employee moves on to another task.

Meanwhile, to one side another customer waits, confidently ready to use the self-service facilities. Before commencing the process, he realizes that to the left-side of the equipment a money note is still jutting out from the slot. The previous user has overlooked this.

However, before the former customer leaves, he is called to, and reminded to not leave his money behind. The customer is pleased, and grateful for the call, stating 'this is very kind of you; we all cannot afford to lose money!'

Here the hand of faith even from a stranger plays an essential role. This situation could have turned out so much more differently, had the stranger decided to take the money for himself.

Where else does faith play its role in our daily life? Lots of little things come to mind. Faith can tip the scales, either verbally or in written form, when what is promised, fails to deliver. When all sorts of excuses are offered around forgetfulness or changed circumstances or unsuitable intentions the expected outcome has changed.

When all this occurs, there is only the hand of faith left, to cover such human failure. The belief is that embarrassment will take hold in the aftermath.

Friendship too builds on faith, as does family relations. Much is excusable here, where faith acts like a binding agent, to positive outcomes.

The hand of faith operates without pre-set conditions. An easy going, relaxed faith leans more towards something like a 'lotto-win', whereas a profound faith involves an unconditional helping hand offered to others. It can be difficult to avoid the perception that individuals operate with their own self-interest in mind, and that others can feel that what was agreed upon becomes forgotten.

In such cases, playing it cool can only help a hand offered in faith, to be interpreted correctly.

When driving in traffic, we all believe that we will arrive at our destination. This is the faith in the car, and our skills, and our attention. Even in the event of an accident, we have faith that the outcome will be not without hope.

Every single passenger of an aircraft believes or has faith that the plane will answer the pilot's commands. Everybody's fate lies in the hands of the pilots, and we believe that they will honour this faith.

Somehow differently runs the hand of faith in politics. Here words and actions have a struggle to find a shared common ground. Despite this, we trust that our faith will not be forgotten.

Faith should not conflict with other strong interests. In the end, the hand of faith when offered, must determine the outcome, and avoid self-interest. We have so much to lose if the hand of faith is denied.

Chapter 50

SOMETHING YOU SHOULD KNOW ABOUT ME

It is also known : "Curiosity killed the cat ." Why would you need to know this one thing about me? This is difficult, as can we ever truly know enough about ourselves, without selecting that one special thing that we need you to know? In addition this runs the risk of attempting to play one's cards too close to one's chest without really knowing the outcome.

In reality, the interest concerning other people is best dealt with by a careful observation from the perspective of distance. Standing back, watching and forming understandings about the person of interest. A more realistic knowledge about another person usually emerges when words embrace the impressions formed, are then put into understandings. We should ask ourselves finally when we believe we know something about the other person, what's the use of it? How close have we come in such a case to interference into private matters?

Having raised the concerns of retaining privacy, there are times when it can amount to survival to know some 'extra' information about either ourselves, or others. In the school of real life, there are the examples of occasions when knowing an extra something would have made a lot of difference to a day's activity.

To clarify by example, let me tell you a story of two friends who some years ago arranged with their girlfriends to go on a tour in their collapsible boat on the local river one Saturday morning. With four people in a small boat, it didn't take long for the boat to commence swaying uncontrollably from side to side, so that its four passengers made a direct entry into the water.

It only became apparent on the entry into the water that the girlfriend of one of them, could not swim at all. Stone-like the young woman disap-peared to the bottom of the river. The urgency of needing to pull her up was the uppermost thought of the remaining three, along with keeping themselves afloat by their swimming efforts.

Only now it had become apparent who could swim and who could not. One thing was for sure; all four had initially entered the boat voluntarily. Perhaps things would have been slightly different if it had become known that one of them was not water proof. She had nothing better on her mind at the end, to hurl strong abuse at her saviours. This boat tour had very quickly come to an end, and everybody knew much more about each other in real terms.

Who was now at fault that somebody got almost killed ? On one hand could cautious curiosity at the right moment have also helped a better outcome with the boat tour. On the other hand, the quintessence is : Curiosity has more than one face, not necessarily the one of a kill.

Chapter 51

THE OLD HOUSE

.....across the street had been vacant for so long.
No doubt ghosts have taken over accommodation
in it, because regular inhabitants could possibly
not feel here at home. And why is that so ?

More grey than originally white paint is visibly peeling off. Shutters on the side of the windows are neither all properly secured in their open position, nor are some completely shut.

When the wind blows out of the sky, the squeaking from its old rusty hinge-joints surpasses repeatedly in only deep cawing single tones the unrhymed windy forces.

The many little glass panels still keep unbroken everything in the house as the shut door at the entrance does. Thin curtain lines barely show from the inside that some living comfort has once occupied this house.

Why does it now look so different from the other houses in its neighbourhood ? Although its roof is immaculate to the eye, its colour does not match a regular roof, it rather stands out in a grey green tone.

Likewise the house, the little land around it follows a neglected impression, Weeds have taken over the grass, only here and there shines little colour through from flowers of a former garden.

The clothes line waits empty in patience for clean washing. Its lines are not straight any more. One or the other hang sadly down. In addition, no motor car has been seen for a long time, waiting next to the old house.

Let's not get impressed one-sided from the outside look of the apparent old house. What obscure life might be still going on in its inside?

In the back of the house reveals a hidden door that in the afternoon, when school has finished, some youngsters, instead of heading straight home from school, they pay the old house a visit, not through the front door but this back door. At a first glance this door springs into the eye, whether it is shut or not, with a number of little round holes in it. Did a shooting took here place which still frightens people in their memories?

Only these school kids know straight away that this door is not locked. Inside, total silence welcomes these intruders straight away, however not for so long. The silence is broken with possibly much nonsense, which at home nor at school would be easily tolerated. Here nobody keeps an eye on them when they hide and seek from one room into another one. Even a ball has joint in this hocus-pocus.

Now is the time that ghosts play their role. Moving shadows from outside moving clouds in the sky also rush occasionally through a window into inside. Only a gaping void fills the rooms, while the kids and the shades try to chase each other. At least this way, life has returned into the old house, even when it was only occasionally during a school day for a short while.

At home waited usually a warning for the youngsters for coming late home from school. The old house on the other side returns regularly to its complete unspoiled silence. What is left behind, are the ghosts who can easily move in and out, continuing their own games, whenever the back door is occasionally forgotten to be completely shut.

Why is all this so that the old house has been vacant for so long ? Who hates whom here ? The old house the people, or the people the old house ? Also here only time will tell.

Chapter 52

STOP WORRYING ABOUT SPILLED MILK

Who today can still experience that very real connection with something from their past, and remember it as if it were today? Here for instance, where milk comes from can still amaze our young city folk. I think back to my younger days in the 1950's and what I learned about this subject and present it here to you, the reader, as an amusing experience. At this time, life was basic and simple, allowing the small things like milking a cow by hand to become an enriching life experience.

Mooing sounds come from the cowshed on the farm where I am staying, almost exactly to the minute, regardless of whether it is a weekday or Sunday. It is always 6 o'clock sharp in the morning, and peace and quiet have fled with the night. Daylight hasn't yet gained the upper hand, but deep white snow in the upper valley with its rising hillsides is sending its ghostly veil of light over the land.

The continued mooing tells the farmer's family it's time to get out of bed. It's a bed which has thick comfortable quilts and a snug hold on us. The cold of the night still hangs around, which means it's hard to keep warm, while performing those first morning duties. I am having a farm holiday, and I didn't want to miss the opportunity to boast about previous farm experiences.

The farmer's daughter, who by the way was not only around my age but charming and beautiful, too, lured me with her smile into the cowshed and asked me to help her milk their four cows. To get started properly, a shiny stainless bucket was placed under the first cow, right under its almost bursting udder. This was not before any cow manure was removed from the floor, and clean straw spread with the welcome touch of the hand of the farmer's daughter. The cow's swollen udder showed a lot of milk. The milking process could now start.

The farmer's daughter knew how to gently touch and prepare the teats for the milk to flow into the bucket underneath. The cow recognized the process as well as the person behind the bucket without failure. After milk was running into the bucket for about a minute or so, the farmer's daughter addressed me from the opposite side underneath the round cow stomach. 'This is how it's done, you show me now, if you can do the milking too. You had better bend down and for your own safety don't get too close to either the cow's body or its hooves. If you help me, we will gain time to be together. Would you like that?'

Both my hands carefully reached the cow's teats underneath the udder. Just touching the teats was obviously enough to upset the cow. As quick as lightening the hooves hit back in all directions, luckily just missing me. The bucket with milk however got a direct hit, flying away through the air and spilling all the contents over the floor.

'Here you are! The cow obviously doesn't like you! The milk is wasted. There is however no need to worry about it. Nobody was injured, and we have learned a very important lesson today, and that is that the cow can be very selective about the person who is milking her. I won't tell Dad that we lost the milk. It won't bring back the milk anyway. For me, it's no surprise that townies can't milk a cow. When you go home again, you'll forget this and me anyway. Am I right?'

"I promise to write you a card when I'm back at home" was all I could think to say to her comments.

After this incident no other cows in the shed had to deal with a foreigner anymore. Continuous chewing sounds came from out of the hayracks and the morning continued on as usual, while I explored the farm lands on ski. The farmer's family spent their day with indoor duties which were reserved mostly for the long cold hours of a freezing snowy day during winter. On holidays, there is enough time to leave all worries behind.

THE BEGINNING & THE END OF ALL STORIES

A mother brings us into this world
And at 20 we start living,
Full of delight, ahead we are looking.
From 30 on we set us a goal
Which at 40 we hope to achieve,
Here energy can help us a lot,
Until 50 it can last if it is not lost,
Then quality of life comes in,
Because 60 is ringing in,
Finally time receives its appreciation
And friendship is calling for its attention,
Unnoticed the 70-ies turn up,
For wine and peace the thumbs go up,
From the 80-ies beauty pleases us,
Family spoils and pampers us,
The 90-ies wait gently and silent
And at 100 wisdom weaves its spell over us.

www.ingramcontent.com/pod-product-compliance
Lightning Source LLC
Chambersburg PA
CBHW030552080526
44585CB00012B/348